Real Talk About Classroom Management

I would not have become the teacher I am without Dr. Orletta Nguyen, a brilliant teacher, and my mentor for many years. You lit my teaching fire and it continues to shine brightly. You inspired my way of thinking and I dedicate this book to you. Thank you.

Real Talk About Classroom Management

50 Best Practices That Work and Show You Believe in Your Students

Serena Pariser

CORWIN
A SAGE Publishing Company

FOR INFORMATION:

Corwin

A SAGE Company

2455 Teller Road

Thousand Oaks, California 91320

(800) 233-9936

www.corwin.com

SAGE Publications Ltd.

1 Oliver's Yard

55 City Road

London EC1Y 1SP

United Kingdom

SAGE Publications India Pvt. Ltd.

B 1/I 1 Mohan Cooperative Industrial Area

Mathura Road, New Delhi 110 044

India

SAGE Publications Asia-Pacific Pte. Ltd.

3 Church Street

#10-04 Samsung Hub

Singapore 049483

Acquisitions Editor: Ariel Bartlett Curry

Development Editor: Desirée A. Bartlett

Editorial Assistant: Jessica Vidal

Production Editor: Tori Mirsadjadi

Copy Editor: Cate Huisman

Typesetter: C&M Digitals (P) Ltd.

Proofreader: Gretchen Treadwell

Indexer: Robie Grant

Cover and Interior Designer: Scott Van Atta

Marketing Manager: Brian Grimm

Printed in the United States of America

ISBN: 978-1-5443-1775-5

This book is printed on acid-free paper.

Certified Chain of Custody
Promoting Sustainable Forestry
www.sfiprogram.org
SFI-01268

SFI label applies to text stock

18 19 20 21 22 10 9 8 7 6 5 4 3 2 1

Contents

Part 4. Other Adults as Resources   144

Part 5. Spins That Will Wow Your Students   184

Part 6. Keeping Yourself Sane 224

Prelude

. . . .

I'll tell it to you like it really is: teacher to teacher. I'll share *real* best practices that worked time after time, *real* anecdotes to illustrate the best practices, *real* conversations I've had with my students and *real* classroom management scenarios I've experienced in my classroom. The only aspect of the book that isn't real is the student names. I would like to share what I have learned with those who are in need or perhaps just curious to build on what they already know.

The first classroom management strategy I tried in my first year was good old-fashioned yelling. I figured if I could get my voice louder and stronger than theirs, I could startle them into listening. It's really all I could think to do with a rowdy class of twenty-nine sixth graders. I eventually realized yelling is only a short-, very short-term and detrimental solution.

The first time I realized yelling can be detrimental, not only to a classroom but also to your health, was around the middle of my very first year in the classroom. I noticed my ears would ache after class. The pain became so unbearable that I eventually went to an ear doctor. The doctor looked in my ears and told me both of my ear drums were very swollen, which was causing the pain. He asked what I did for a living and I told him I was a sixth-grade teacher. He chuckled, and replied, "That's why your ear drums are swollen." I was put on steroidal medication to alleviate the pain and swelling. My ears did return to normal, but it was literally a painful wakeup call to how much I was raising my voice in the classroom. Something had to change. If my ears were in pain, I couldn't even imagine how my students felt in my classroom. Something was off, and I was determined to find a better way to teach. This is where my quest to find the best practices in teaching began.

I've always considered myself fearless. I bungee jumped and skydived in New Zealand on the same day, rafted through Class 4 rapids, free fall jumped from casinos in Las Vegas, snorkeled with sharks, backpacked solo through Australia, Costa Rica, Turkey, Namibia, Botswana, and five other countries, canoed down deadly hippopotamus-infested waters in Zimbabwe, and jumped in frozen lakes for fun—twice. None of these adventures comes close to the accomplishment I felt when I finally figured out what makes classrooms work. Most of us, including myself, make mistakes trying to figure out what works. Most new teachers have little help, a few teaching books, and maybe a classroom management course or two to guide them. I'd like to give back to the profession and tell you everything I know that has worked over and over again with students, and direct you to everything that most teachers say works. I'm here to make it easier for you.

I am not claiming to have the right way to teach. What makes teaching so difficult, so complex, and so beautiful is that there are many right ways, and more are being discovered every day. However, many best practices form a common thread among good teachers. I am sharing my knowledge and insights about what has worked for me and my peers. What is revealed in this book is just the tip of the iceberg, and it took me seven-plus years to figure it out through trial and error, through tears and triumph. I hope to save you some of the mistakes I made and share with you the many joys I had in the classroom and how I came to have them. I wrote this for you, so you can spend less time on the errors and discovering what works for you and your students. Many of my practices are inspired by *real questions* teachers would ask me as we were walking down the hallway, during lunch, during my prep period, after school, or through e-mail. Every time a teacher asked me a question, I immediately started developing a new practice for this book, because if one person is asking, there's every chance that other people have the same question.

Learning these insights took me years of practice, trying every-and-any teaching method, reading the research, working closely with a mentor, and working in challenging school settings. Through my growing determination, reflective practices, curiosity about what works in teaching, passion to always be better, and love of the students, I earned Teacher of the Year in my school and was awarded a Fulbright Distinguished Teacher grant to coach educators in Botswana, Africa, on student engagement, technology, interdisciplinary problem based units, and student-centered lessons. I've coached teachers in Kathmandu, Nepal, on student-centered lessons and empowering students. I've worked with students from Eastern Europe and Russia and taught K–12 classes in Turkey.

What I found from coaching teachers and working with students around the world is that even through language barriers, there are universal best practices that consistently bring success to teachers and students. I knew I had to share what I learned and accomplished with others. These positive and powerful moments are what got me up way too early in the morning and what kept me working countless hours after school. I hope you can use this book to build on my experiences for even greater successes in your own classrooms and homes.

Let me break it down for you with a few *real* statistics. Times are changing.

According to a study conducted by Child Trends (2015), there are five critical skills most likely to increase the odds of success across all outcomes, and which employers expect employees to have: social skills, communication skills, and higher-order thinking skills (including problem solving, critical thinking, and decision making); supported by the intrapersonal skills of self-control and positive self-concept (Lippman, Ryberg, Carney, & Moore, 2015).

Here's another real-world statistic to support this: It has been reported that 85 percent of those who lose their jobs are terminated because of inadequate social skills (DeRoche, 2013). "Employers also want new hires to have technical knowledge related to the job, but that's not nearly as important as good teamwork, decision-making and communication skills, and the ability to plan and prioritize work" (Adams, 2014, ¶1). Today, companies are hiring people who can work independently just as well as they can with others. Obedience is not valued as much as other 21st century skills, which has teachers rethinking how this translates to classroom management. How do we prepare our students for the real world?

When we think of classroom management, we traditionally think of ways to keep students quiet, well behaved, and on task. However, in order to prepare them for today's world, we should think of classroom management as guiding students to work collaboratively, communicate with each other, and listen to their classmates' thoughts and opinions. Classroom management is about building students up, not breaking them down. This means we teachers are starting to shift our own perspective.

> We should think of classroom management as guiding students to work collaboratively, communicate with each other, and listen to their classmates' thoughts and opinions.

Perhaps you've already heard of a few of these best practices. Or, perhaps you have your own twist on the practices, and those are perfect to share with your colleagues in the discussion questions at the end of each chapter. The point is that each of these parts warrants discussion, because they are all critical parts of what makes learners engaged, confident, empowered, and independent learners.

Why Teach?

They say the person you fall in love with should bring out the best in you, making your light shine. The same goes for the job you fall in love with. Teaching is one of the most vulnerable professions out there. It should make your best qualities shine, lighting you up from the inside out. Teaching did this for me. It brought out characteristics in me that I did not know existed. Just like anything you open your heart and mind to, it brought out the best in me but also exposed my raw weaknesses. However, those moments when my weaknesses were most glaring motivated me to work toward becoming a better teacher.

The kids out there need you. There might be times you mess up a lesson or a conversation with a student. That's more than okay, it's expected—you're human. It's all part of the process. You'll have students who need your support because their parents both work two jobs, or maybe they need you as a role model because they don't have one. Or just maybe, you'll be the kindest adult they know. As educators, we get to be exactly what they need, complete with all our imperfections. How lucky are we?

There is something special about teaching. We all have our own reasons that drew us to this profession, and they are all unique. I'm not sure if any of my teachers from middle or high school know I became a teacher. I'm pretty sure if you told them that I was a teacher, it would surprise them. Until college, I was never particularly motivated as a student. I flew under the radar and did just enough not to draw attention to myself. I wonder what was going on all of those other years in the classroom when I was passing notes to my friends. (I filled an entire box of notes. My friends and I earned an *A* in note writing, not note taking.) Having friends was more important to me than learning. My junior year of college is when my light switch went on and I actually started feeling smart. I was a different student.

My history of academic apathy is probably the single most important factor in my success as a teacher. I understand why students get bored, feel unengaged, fall asleep, get rowdy, et cetera. I get it. But I also know how to convert that energy into engagement and excitement in the classroom.

I bet you can't find one teacher who hasn't shed a tear of joy the first time she found success in a student. If you look around any teacher's desk, you'll probably see a thank-you card from a student displayed. These cards bring us so much joy. That's why I've included actual quotes from real students in the beginning of each part. Students remember the way we make them feel. You'll see the light switch turn on in a child's eyes when you explain a concept well and they get it. When you ask teachers what they do, they'll usually smile as they explain what grade and subject they teach. You can't say that about many other professions. This book will show you ways to make your students feel good while learning. The emotional element is a significant part of the process for teachers and student alike.

There's a time in your teaching career when you feel lucky just to be a person in your students' lives every day, because they are phenomenal. And there's a point where your students, even when they are difficult, will feel lucky just to be able to be in your class. With love, patience, skill, and creativity, you will actually be working and changing a person's life, in your classroom, every day.

There's going to be a point where you are working way too hard, and that's where I'd like to come in and help take some of the load off of you. Whatever classroom management frustration you've ever had in your classroom, I've most likely been there. I'm listening, I understand, and I can help. To all the teachers reading this book: Thank you for joining our team. We need people like you.

—Serena

Acknowledgments

Thank you Gompers Preparatory Academy and Vincent Riveroll for showing me that one person can make a difference and miracles do happen when you believe in a child. Thank you for building me up to the teacher I have become. GPA is one remarkable school that is truly closing the achievement gap.

Thank you to my #1 fans: This book is a product of a lot of motivation from many different people. I'd like to thank my father, Ben Pariser, and step-mother, Melanie, for walking with me every step of the way, spending countless hours helping me revise and edit, keeping me motivated, and staying optimistic. Thank you to Aunt Carla and Uncle Ron for spending countless hours supporting me and reading drafts. Thanks to Aunt Ellen Pariser for all of the support and wisdom you have from many successful years in the classroom. Thank you to Melissa Pariser, my brother, Joe Pariser, and friend, Joe Schlesser, for reading my drafts. Thank you to my older brother and sister-in-law, Robert Pariser and Pam Pariser, for pushing me to be better tomorrow. I hope Sam, Skylar, Sloane, and Aria have inspirational teachers in their lives. Thank you to Joel Sprechman for giving me the idea to write a book. Thank you, Chris McCarry, Carolyn King, and Karen Reddick, for your ideas when I needed help. Thank you to Adriana for giving me advice from a student's point of view. You are wise beyond your years. Thank you to my Panera Bread writer's group who put their own time and energy into revising and editing my work. Thank you to Eric Karpinski for your inspiration many years ago. Thank you, Mia Adriano, for offering your house as a quiet space to write when I needed most. Thank you to the lovely and talented Mia Regala and paper-scraps.com for the artistic vector diagrams in the book. Thank you to my Tales From the Classroom crew (Christina, Sandeep, Alicia, Joe, Jimmy, Karen, Juan, and Kimberly) for giving me a forum to share my crazy classroom tales. I'm glad you convinced me to save them for something one day. Thank you Catherine Beck and Melissa Pariser for your endless feedback and teacher perspectives. Thank you to my blog editor, Andrew Rossillo, for helping me get to where I am with your editing skills and your words of encouragement and support. Thank you Skye, Kristin, and Kate for being my #1 support fans. Thank you to my lovely manuscript editor, Ariel Bartlett Curry.

To the teachers I met around the world during my travels, thank you for sharing your stories with me to use in this book. To all of the teachers around the United States that I reached out to for this book for your words of advice and stories from the classroom, thank you. Your stories are inspirational.

Thank you, Dr. Edward DeRoche, for appearing in my life unexpectedly and showing me a whole new world in education. Thank you to my mother, Issy Pariser, for loving me every step of the way and reminding me that "the mango does not grow without the tree." And to the strongest and most stubborn person I know, my ninety-eight-year old pop pop, Dr. Sid Pariser, who would never let me leave anything halfway finished and has shown me unconditional love my entire life. To my grandmother, Selma Pariser, who showed me that being yourself is the only way to shine and the world will love you for who you are. And to the most valuable teachers of all: Every one of my former students (especially the most challenging—you know who you are)—you taught me, believed in me, and pushed to become a better teacher. Thank you, all. I hope I have inspired you in return. And to my readers, I challenge you to share your goals once they are more than a thought.

About the Author

Serena Pariser, MA, has 12 years' experience teaching in public schools (including charter schools) from kindergarten through twelfth grade. She has taught in some of the most challenging school settings from coast to coast, including a boarding school for students from fifteen different Indian tribes in South Dakota, North Dakota, and Nebraska. In addition to her extensive experience in urban school settings, she also has experience in affluent schools, and has truly seen all sides of education. Most of her full-time teaching experience is at the middle school level, although she has experience in high school and elementary school settings. She earned her bachelor's degree in education at The Pennsylvania State University and a master's degree in educational technology from San Diego State University. She has been a teacher, teacher coach, and curriculum designer, and has held leadership positions in school settings. Serena was humbled to be recognized as Teacher of the Year at Gompers Preparatory Academy.

Serena has been invited to present at three consecutive Character Matters conferences at University of San Diego about integrating character education into the Common Core curriculum. Furthermore, she copresented at the 2015 Diving Deep: Common Core and Next Generation Science Standards conference at the University of California at San Diego. She will be presenting at both the northern and southern California 2018 Good Teaching conferences on the topic of classroom management. Serena was a three-year member of the advisory board at the Character Education Resource Center at University of San Diego. She later transitioned into the role of an assistant to the director of Character Education Resource Center and then to lead administrator for the 2017 twenty-first annual Character Matters Conference, which brings together administrators and teachers from all over the country. Serena was selected to be an evaluator for National Schools of Character, where she evaluated elementary schools' character education programs and determined if they were eligible to be a National School of Character.

In addition to her educational work in the United States, Serena has expanded her educational knowledge around the globe. She coached teachers and modeled best practices and engagement strategies in Kathmandu, Nepal, and also taught in rural parts of Turkey. Serena was selected as a US Ambassador with Fulbright Distinguished Teachers Award, which gave her an opportunity to coach teachers in Botswana on engagement strategies, smart technology uses, and best practices in the classroom.

Serena has a national audience of educators on social media and on her website at www.serenapariser.com, where she publishes educational articles for teachers around the country and globe. She works full-time as assistant director of field experience at University of San Diego, where she supervises the field training experiences of teachers entering the profession. She also instructs master's and undergraduate classes for student teachers at University of San Diego.

My First Year

. . . .

[Warning: Sensitive Material]

Expectations? Of course, I had expectations as a first year teacher teaching in a notoriously rough area of West Philadelphia. They were simple: Try to keep the kids from fighting and don't cry in front of the class. I was where many first year teachers find themselves—in survival mode. One particular day of my first year is ingrained in my memory.

My class is out of control. Twenty-nine sixth graders are laughing and pointing at each other. They know I can't stop them. A wadded up paper ball flies through the air, followed by a shriek from its unexpected target. A direct hit. The target looks around the room and threatens retaliation to everybody in that vicinity. I lack the energy and know-how to address the escalating chaos. I am focused on the student who is sitting at his desk shaking and rocking back and forth. He has completely lost it because the other students directly in front of me are ridiculing him. I cannot stop it. There are too many of them. I am the one versus many. He is shaking and crying. Some students notice; some do not. My mind is racing: *Wait, do I have to report this? How do I report this? Does he have a weapon? How do I get someone to help me right now? What will they think about this class? I'm so embarrassed. How many minutes left of this period? Oh God, what if he tries to get back at them during class?* A familiar lump builds in the back of my throat and begins to creep up. I feel the tears welling up with the promise of streaming down my face. *Oh God, don't cry. That will be it. You'll be the teacher that cried. Don't cry. Don't cry. HELP!* One student is asleep in the back. Another is trying to pay attention to my math lesson, but I know it is only because he feels bad for me. I'm not sure if any of them know that I am teaching, or trying to teach, a lesson. This was my beginning.

By no means do I assume you have been there, nor do I wish this upon you. But perhaps you have had similar experiences. I chose to work in this part of West Philadelphia my first year teaching. I wasn't always skilled at what I did, but I survived it and used these experiences to become wiser about teaching.

Around my seventh year in the classroom, a sixth-grade student stopped me in the hall and said confidently, "I want to be in your class in two years. My friends tell me it's really good." That started being a regular occurrence. Students who weren't placed in my class that year would lurk by the door before and after class and ask if there were any openings. This type of feedback means more to us than any formal evaluation, because our students are our true evaluators.

I started to notice that I wasn't coming home most days defeated. I was elated, tired but elated, after work. And the days I was coming home frustrated became fewer, and the days I was coming home elated became the norm. I felt excited and energized when I was teaching, and I was actually having fun and smiling, rather than always on guard for the next student misbehavior. When you have this shift, it's a feeling that our students sense, and in turn, they let down their guard. You and your students become a solid team.

When we keep a growth mindset, stay attuned to current best practices in teaching, and take risks out of our comfort zone in the classroom, it's inevitable that we grow as teachers. Even when we feel like we are not growing some days, most likely we are. For me, it took a strong growth mindset, experiencing failures as well as successes, trying every teaching method I could find, finding my groove, constantly reading the research, learning through a mentor, and working in challenging school settings to try to hone my craft. I felt I had to share what I learned with others, so maybe you don't have to work quite as hard as you are right now, or maybe I can help you come home a little less tired. This book is for you, the teacher. Hopefully you can experience some or more of the successes I had in the classroom. These moments are what kept me working countless hours after school. I was thirsty for any teacher tricks and successful strategies I could get my hands on, and I'd like to share what I've learned with you. Let's do this together.

Teachers need to know this. It's really good. The book is not only great for teachers but for parents who can't seem to control their teenagers. It gives teachers new ideas that they probably haven't thought of before. It would work for parents, too, or for anyone that wants to teach kids in a very marvelous and productive way. It's the same whether you are teaching or whether you are a parent. I think this book is really beneficial, even for the students, because it can help you understand how teachers think and that they don't always want to get us in trouble! This book really had me thinking about all these tricks about how teachers get us to start working.

—Eighth-Grade Student

PART 1
FIRST WEEKS OF SCHOOL

A Memorable Day 1. . . .

On Day 1 of 9th grade history, another teacher walked into the classroom and asked to borrow some paper, and our teacher completely flipped out and made a scene. We all watched in disbelief. Then, after it was over, she asked us to write down what we saw, including every detail, from the color of the shirt the other teacher was wearing to the length of time the confrontation went on, and to include exact quotes from the interaction. We read all of them afterward, and there were so many variations of what everyone witnessed. Then she went on to say that much of history is like that as well. I'll never forget it.

—Amy, age 38

What do the first weeks of school have to do with classroom management?

Everything. First of all, we want to be prepared and not only on time, but early, so my first year experience doesn't happen to you. The first weeks of school will establish routines in your classroom and set your expectations for behavior and participation in place, and this will be the time your students form good habits in your classroom. This is also the time you will start to build a relationship based on mutual respect with students and set boundaries and structures. A strong first few weeks of the year almost always predicts a strong school year. Make these few weeks count.

BEST PRACTICE #1

Make Day 1 About the Students

The first day of school should be all about the students. We need to learn their names as fast as possible. The sooner we know their names, the more we care about them. That's what they're thinking. I promise. Referring to your seating chart will help you learn the names the quickest. My seating chart is virtually attached to my hands the first few weeks of school, until I learn all of the student names. Make sure the seating chart is always on a clipboard you walk around the classroom with. The students don't really know what is on your clipboard, so the fact that you are addressing them by name will be impressive to them. Other adults in your room should have a copy of the seating chart too, so they know names as well.

In the first two days, you may not have a seating chart yet, and students may still be enrolling in the school or your class. However, you can still start learning student names in a few creative ways.

Tips for Learning Students' Names

Learning Students' Names Method #1 (Basic): If you're a little hesitant and would rather take a conservative approach to learning names, that's fine. My mentor taught me an effortless trick: Just have the students take an index card and fold it in half on their desks. Have them write their first name as large as possible on half the card, and display the name facing you. They keep the cards and put them up as soon as they get into your class. This will work for the first few days. Then, make a seating chart as soon as possible to get a handle on the names fast. You could also use name tags, but index cards are reusable and easier on your wallet. Most schools provide index cards to teachers at the beginning of the school year.

Learning Students' Names Method #2: Use student pictures. Most attendance programs now will make seating charts with student pictures on them. If you don't want to take the time to construct one, you can either cut and paste the student pictures on your seating chart, or keep a reference of student pictures on your clipboard, behind your seating chart.

Learning Students' Names Method #3 (Advanced): I read this in W. Michael Kelley's *Rookie Teaching for Dummies* (2003) and use it every year. Don't let the title deter you; I read that book in my fifth year of teaching and used many new ideas I found. I started using this technique in Year 5, only because I had never heard of it before. I would caution newer teachers against using it if it's your first year in the classroom. The students get a kick out of it, and it's really effective for learning names. It also shows the students that you are creative, and they may never know what to expect.

1. Start at one edge of your classroom and ask the student her first name.

2. Move on to the student behind her.

3. Go back and forth a few times between the two of them, repeating their names as you look into their faces.

4. Move on to a third student, repeat the name, and review all the names you've learned so far.

5. Repeat this process until you learn the entire class, and then spend some time picking out students at random and trying to remember their names.

6. When you feel comfortable with the names, turn your back, and ask the students to change desks.

My goal was always to find out about my students on the first day (make it about them). Show them you care who they are as learners. I like to do an activity to get them talking to each other and problem solving. Remember, they are as scared as you are. They want to know about you, but they also want to know each other. You will need your class to be friendly with each other to have a productive year, so it pays off if they can learn to communicate with a bit of structure to enjoy speaking with and learning from each other. This is why structured team-building or icebreaker activities are priceless on this day.

On the first day you want your students to smile, be able to communicate with each other, and start raising hands. Save the rest for later. The icebreaker activities I enjoyed the most required students to be up and out of their seats, around the room, and trying to solve a puzzle in a group or team. There are tons of these activities online, in books, or in the minds of your colleagues. A book I recommend for icebreakers and team-building activities that can carry throughout the year is *Thiagi's 100 Favorite Games* (Thiagarajan, 2006). This book is filled with team-building and icebreaker activities for learners, from grade-school age up to adult, to help build a community of leaders and critical thinkers in your classroom. My copy lives on the bookshelf beside my desk.

Figure 1.1 shows the traditional way of doing Day 1, as well as better way that will engage your students.

In Best Practice #5, you'll see why having students speak to one another on Day 1 will help you build a seating chart the first week. You have to see a glimpse of their personalities. Day 2 is when they can begin to take notes, learn the classroom rules, understand your expectations and consequences, and get ready to learn. Day 1 shows them you are curious about *them*, and you want to hear *their* voices and learn *their* names.

Figure 1.1   Engaging Your Students on Day 1

OLD WAY OF DOING DAY 1	FRESH AND ENGAGING IDEAS FOR DAY 1
Teacher goes over class rules and expectations.	Students do a collaborative icebreaker or structured collaborative activity. Teacher saves rules and expectations for Day 2
Students leave with an idea of the teacher's personality.	Teacher is more interested in seeing the personalities of the students.
Students do not know their classmates and may be resistant to collaborate the next day.	Students start to know their classmates and collaboration is easier the next day.
Student voice is not heard.	Student voice is heard.
Students leave the room understanding rules and expectations.	Students leave the room smiling and excited for the next day of class. Teacher goes over rules and expectations on Day 2.

Your turn

1. What is one of your favorite icebreaker activities? Why do you like it so much?

I'm thinking of getting my students to break up into groups to build something.

2. What message does doing a team-building or icebreaker activity on Day 1 relay to your students?

Team-building activity relays the message that the class is a collaborative team where the students' opinion and ideas matter.

3. Why is it important to have students talking to each other on Day 1 in a structured activity? How will this facilitate student collaboration in your classroom?

This will establish the expectation that I encourage my students to collaborate in the class.

4. Think about a successful icebreaker you've done in the past. What were some of the long-term positive results that came out of doing that icebreaker?

It's always fun learning something interesting about the other people that I go to school or that I work with

Get Respect—and Fast

All of my years as a student I went through a countless number of teachers. I have had cool teachers, strict teachers, laid-back teachers. I have always thought, *I wish I could have a teacher who knows how to be all of those, when they need* to.

—Sammy, Grade 9

I chose to complete my four-month student teaching assignment at a boarding school in rural Pierre, South Dakota, with one hundred percent Native American students from the surrounding reservations. I've always been attracted to a challenge. I remember the first time the classroom teacher allowed me to administer my own quiz. Finally, I had my own class, if only for a few minutes. I handed out the papers and proceeded to walk around the room as I was giving directions. One eighth-grade girl yelled in a snarky tone, "Hey, what's your first name anyway?" I replied trying to sound as authoritative as possible, "Serena, but *you* have to call me Ms. Pariser!" I shot her a look that I thought screamed, "Don't mess with me." She must have interpreted it as "I'm going to demand your respect and you're going to give it to me." That rarely works, unless you're looking for respect out of intimidation. As a student teacher, I was anything but intimidating.

She thought for a second and then yelled "Hey, Serena!"

I fell into her trap and replied, "Ms. Pariser!" She laughed and yelled even louder "Serena, Serena, Serena!" This went back and forth for a little. My face was boiling red. I have my final I'm-going-to-teach-you comeback, "MS. PARISER! YOU ARE A STUDENT!"

BAM.

A spiral bound one-hundred-sheet notebook hit the side of my face. She had thrown it at me, with perfect aim, in a successful attempt to shut me up. My eyes started to water in fright. Did a student really just throw a notebook at my face? Did it really just hit me? Am I bleeding? What does the rest of the class think? Did they see? I started to tremble. I said in my calmest voice "Call security." I was shaking. This is how I learned to not demand respect. You have to earn it.

Does Amazon sell Respect? It seems like some teachers have it from their students, and some do not. How do they do it? Let me start by saying if the students respect and like you as a person, your job will be a lot easier. Unlike a boss who doesn't like an employee, you can't "fire" a student. You can spend your entire year trying to fix a fractured relationship that is broken due to lack of respect. Here are some guidelines to help earn the respect of your students (not an easy task):

First: You are _part_ of the class. It's not you versus the class.

Is your goal to get the kids to listen to you or to help each of them succeed? Think hard about this. Do you and the kids have the same goals in mind? Now, you may be thinking, *Yes, but how do I help them succeed if they don't even listen when I am talking?* You're not the only one who's been on the verge of tears. I soon learned that when there is a battle in the classroom (you vs. them), they can and will overpower you. They outnumber you. Scary thought, right? The secret is that you can't let them know that. That's the difference between an unsuccessful teacher and a successful teacher. Successful teachers know this, and work with their students. Unsuccessful teachers seem to fall into the trap of testing their power, using a loud voice to try to overpower. Power struggles rarely work in the long run. They lead to intimidation, which doesn't create an ideal learning environment. Yes, I've been overpowered. I've had students walk out of my classroom, curse in my face, and laugh when I discipline them. It's not a pleasant situation when a student or whole class shows disrespect. It's also hard to earn respect back once it's lost. However, once the students trust—yes, trust—that you have their interests in mind, they will let their guard down and get ready for the educational journey. They will _want_ you to lead them. They will _ask_ you what they are going to learn today. They will _give up_ the fight, because they realize you and they are all on the same side. How do you do this? Don't tell them; show them that you have their interests in mind.

> If you want them to take their jobs seriously as students, do your job by being prepared to teach.

Always be well prepared for class.

o Be on time/Early
o Have well-planned lessons

Be yourself.

Tips for Earning the Respect of Your Students

- **Focus on Your Goal.** Whatever you focus on is what will thrive in the classroom. If you focus on negative behaviors, that is what will thrive. If you focus on classroom rules, they will learn the rules, but when will they learn content? My advice: Always have your lesson prepared. Focus on the learning. Show them that learning is always the first priority. That is your job. If you want them to take seriously their jobs as students, do your job by being prepared to teach. If you focus on your lesson plan, you will feel confident, and the rest will follow.

- **Let Students Know You Believe in Their Success.** Tell your students that you believe in their success. Do you think they will rise to the occasion if you challenge them? Here's a secret: If you believe in them, and you tell them so, they will believe in themselves. If you don't believe that your students will succeed, they won't believe either.

  Example: Nathan, I really want you to do well today. How can I help you with that?

  Instead of: Nathan, you have an F in my class, don't you want to get a good grade? Why can't you behave?

  Both statements show Nathan that he is accountable for his behavior. The first statement, however, shows him you believe in his success and it is his choice how he behaves. You are rooting for him. The second statement puts a student on the defensive, which rarely works. Be smart with your words and work on the relationship. The way you communicate makes a big difference in how you are received by the students.

- **Be the Teacher You Are.** This seems like a simple statement, but I always found it profound. Be your best self inside your class. What excites you that you can use in the classroom to accelerate learning? Use your personality strengths in your teaching. Do you love acting? Then use it in your teaching. Are you a great artist but teaching math? Draw out some math problems! Do you love playing the piano? Why don't you play to the students as they are working? Your strengths are one of the biggest assets in your classroom. I love being silly and playful in life, and for many years I tried to run a very serious class, because I was afraid of doing anything different as a new teacher. Once I brought my silly side to the learning, my students' test scores jumped, they were happier, and I was a happier teacher. We know there are still serious times in the classroom, but we also know when we can laugh together. Weave your personality into the lesson. If you are a golf-loving science teacher, why not bring in your nine irons on the day you teach force? If you do this, you are much more likely to be a better and "real" (as the students like to say) teacher.

- **Work on Your Weaknesses.** In addition to using your strengths to become a real person in the students' eyes, you have to be willing to work on your weaknesses if that is what the students need. Let them know you learned how to do this specifically for them. You are a student as well. Think of yourself as a caretaker. This is the work you have to do outside of school hours (or during your prep period if you're super efficient). This is what your students need. Say there were two inexperienced teachers discussing groupwork. One teacher might say, "Groupwork is just not my thing. They can't handle it. It's easier to just have them work independently." The second teacher may say, "I know groupwork is better for the students and I also know this is my weak spot. I'm going to learn how to do it." Which teacher do you think the students will respect more, and which will have better-prepared, engaging lessons?

- **Use Discipline Sparingly.** If you discipline, do so for a specific purpose, and tell your students why. They will respect your authority and admire that you rarely have to use your power. Anger can be effective only if it is used rarely. Anger used often is completely ineffective. Discipline once, within the first two months of school, and only after you have taught the structures of your classroom. This establishes boundaries. Students need you to be stern when they cross your boundaries. While it may feel cruel, being stern establishes and maintains control. For me, it was usually once every two months. For example, you could address your class with, "Do you remember the classroom rules we discussed (point to them). Do we need something added to address side conversations? I want to make sure we're on the same page. If there's a misunderstanding, I can certainly address that. I know you're not trying to be malicious, but you are in fact breaking a rule." If you do it too much, you do not have control. Learn to pick and choose your battles. I always asked myself, *Is it affecting the learning of the whole class?* If the answer is yes, it is your job to stop the offending behavior. If the answer is no, do not stop the classroom for just one student. It's just not fair to the other students, unless you are using your discipline action as a teachable moment. Your class will respect your authority and admire that you are a teacher who puts student learning at the forefront, rather than showing how powerful you can be as a disciplinarian. They, in turn, will start to put learning at the forefront as well.

Get out of your comfort zone. Learn things that will promote your students' learning.

Your turn

1. What do you think are your teaching strengths? Are they the same as or different from what other teachers have recognized as your strengths? How do you use this information to maximize student learning?

    _____

    _____

    _____

    _____

    _____

2. When is the last time you disciplined a full classroom? Can you remember a teacher who did this? Do you think it worked or not? If not, how could you or that teacher do it differently next time?

    _____

    _____

    _____

    _____

    _____

3. What do you love? Can you bring this to your classroom or teaching so the students can get a better sense of who you are?

    _____

    _____

    _____

    _____

    _____

BEST PRACTICE #3

Set Your Routine and Structures Early—and Keep Them!

If you've ever substitute-taught or covered a colleague's classroom, you know that you can tell a good teacher the moment you walk into his or her class. Even when their teacher isn't there, the students know what do to. They enter a certain way, they go to their seats, they do a certain procedure first, they ask to do certain things and know not to ask for others. This classroom routine shows the teacher set structures early.

Setting structures early almost guarantees a successful year. Let students own the routine. Humans tend to keep habits. Without habit, classroom and life may be exciting, but we start to feel out of place. Give students a habitual way to start and end your class.

Tips for Establishing Classroom Structures

- **Make It Easy.** Make sure your structures are not too tedious. If a student has to get a pencil, does he have to sign ten release forms? Or is there a basket always in the same place that holds pencils? If the structures make sense and show you value the students, then they will work.

(Continued)

(Continued)

- **Consistency Is Key.** Don't change your structures often. Newer teachers sometimes tend to love to change structures. They always think of a new way to make it work. I'm not saying don't ever change structures, but having an established routine works and makes students feel comfortable. Students learn to remember and do daily things automatically. If you keep changing—even if the new structures are better—they'll forget what the newest structure is, and just follow no structure. Decide early on ones that work.

- **Structure the Beginning of Class.** Give structure to the beginning of your class period. Have all the students doing the same type of thing at the beginning of class, kind of like your morning routine. This way, even if they come in groggy, they will know what to do automatically. Do this every day if possible. An example of a great structure is this:

  1. Go directly to your seat and sit.
  2. Place your backpack on the back of your chair or on the floor.
  3. Take out your homework log, and record your homework.
  4. Start doing the warm-up exercise on the board.

Remember to praise them each and every time they follow your routine, no matter how easy it is.

Once you have your class do the same routine for about seven days, the students will get in the habit of doing the same thing again, and the routine will become comforting to them. They will feel success, since they are following the rules.

Routines need to be set as early as possible in Week 1:

- What is the procedure for signing out classroom computers?
- How do you deal with tardy students?
- Have students been assigned computer numbers? This is most effective if computer numbers are on student names on a seating chart.
- How do students sign books out from the classroom?
- What do students do when they need to use the bathroom?
- Where are assignments turned in?
- Where can extra worksheets be found for absent students?
- Where is homework written on the board for students to record?
- What is your classroom policy for student use of cell phones and other electronic devices?

Your turn

1. Look at the previous page's list. What is a structure or routine that you've seen work well in a classroom for one of the items?

   _____

   _____

   _____

   _____

   _____

2. In your opinion, are there any activities or procedures that do not need a structure and/or routine? Why?

   _____

   _____

   _____

   _____

   _____

3. Do you think it's more important to have a routine to begin the class or a routine to end the class or both? Why?

   _____

   _____

   _____

   _____

Speak Student

Your class is a place I look forward to coming to every day.

—Carmen, Grade 9

Even though students are mandated to attend school daily, don't take advantage of that. Strive to make it a place they look forward to coming to. After my third year teaching, a close teacher friend gave me one of the most meaningful presents I have ever received. She handed me a book: *Positive Words, Powerful Results* by Hal Urban (2004).

Inside the front cover was a handwritten note about how teaching is all about what we say and how we say it. This message stayed with me. It took me a few months before I started reading the book. I mean, who could read books for fun with all those papers to grade, right? This book was just the beginning of my journey of realizing that teaching is all about making the students feel good, challenged, successful, and supported. The climate in the classroom begins with your words: what you say and *how* you say it. It is an art and a science. Some of us are born with the ability to *give* not *take* from others with our subconscious choice of words. This wasn't the case for me; I had to learn. The book was one of the most meaningful presents to me because it cracked the door to show me that our words can be our biggest ally or our biggest hurdle to becoming a great teacher.

I can do this now, but I remember a time during my third year of teaching where I failed. I was walking my ninth graders down the hallway and they were supposed to be silent. One notoriously defiant boy continued to talk. I first threatened to make the whole class turn around (secretly hoping I didn't need to go there because I wasn't even sure if they would listen to me enough to turn

18

around). The boy continued to talk away, fearless of my threats. I stopped the class, stuck out my first finger, otherwise known as the teacher finger of shame, and waved it with every word I said.

"STOP TALKING!"

He laughed.

"I SAID, STOP. TALKING!" A bit louder this time, and with a face more red, my head leaned downwards and eyes of fire (or so I thought) staring.

He turned around to not only laugh, but show his classmates he didn't care with a snarky glance. This was probably not the first time a teacher tried to overpower him.

He had zero fear of me, and fear was the emotion I was trying to trigger in him to get obedience. Needless to say, the story ended with my head almost flying off because of all of the blood that had rushed to it, and he eventually stopped talking, but just to get out of the school gates. I lost. He left laughing and I took an aspirin. This story is just one of many of times when I was not "speaking student."

Just writing about this story today is painful. As teachers, we have to be careful not to beat ourselves up for times we might mess up. These are the times when we are learning, and these times will be your biggest teachers.

> We have to be careful not to beat ourselves up for times we might mess up. These are the times when we are learning, and these times will be your biggest teachers.

"I need you to"... statements

Tips for Improving How We Speak to Students

- Use "I" statements. If you want a student to do something, especially when correcting behavior, never say, "*You* need to. . . ." Always start with "*I need you to* . . ." Students can't really argue with an "I" statement. It's very easy for a student to argue with a "you" statement.

- When speaking to a seated student one on one, try to kneel down, so your head is at the level of theirs or below. This is less intimidating for students, and they will be more likely to open up to you.

- Say students' names when speaking to them, but not in a threatening way. People love hearing their own names. In fact, according to Dale Carnegie's *How to Win Friends and Influence People* (1998), "A person's name is to that person the sweetest and most important sound in any language" (p. 83). Dale Carnegie knew how to win people over. This is why this tactic will work for your class.

(Continued)

(Continued)

- Put yourself in your students' shoes. Think of the last time you spoke to your class. Would you appreciate being spoken to like that? If the answer is yes, well done! Great job! You are ahead of where most are, including myself, in Year 1 or 2. I equate the first years of teaching to fighting with a significant other in an unhealthy relationship. You say things you don't mean, you apologize, you lose control at times, you wonder why the other doesn't care about all the preparation you are putting in. However, the great news is that as you become more experienced, you realize that you are on the same team as your students, not on an opposing team. You have more control. Yes, you will still lose your cool, but it happens rarely and for a specific reason. Yes, you will disagree, but you will keep your composure as you see the issue for what it is. Where can you start growing? Speak to the students with respect. They will do what you want them to do more often and because they want to, not because they are afraid of you or sick of hearing you nag.

Respectful comment: "Jorge, I need you to sit down, please."

Disrespectful comment (in the mind of a student): "Sit down or you will have detention."

Helpful language empowers and harmful language breaks students down. The student sees the first one as the teacher doing him a favor—but he sees the second comment as a threat, a challenge: You are using your power to hold over his head that you can give him detention. Ironically, you really could in both cases; you are just making him feel like you are doing him a favor with the first comment.

HELPFUL LANGUAGE	HARMFUL LANGUAGE
I need you to. . . .	You need to. . . .
Do me a favor and sit down. . . .	Sit down NOW!
Can you do me a favor and listen up please?	Why aren't you listening?
Could you please stop talking to your neighbor and listen a bit more closely?	Why can't you stop talking?
"I" statements	"You" statements

I will admit, sometimes you can get faster results with harmful language, but when we do that we are breaking the students down, and they may resent us in the long run.

Your turn

1. Can you remember a teacher who made you feel not good because of the words she used? What did the teacher say, and how did she say it?

   _____

   _____

   _____

   _____

2. Now think of an instructor who made you feel great every time you heard her speak to the class or to you. Do you remember specific words she said or just the way the words made you feel?

   _____

   _____

   _____

   _____

3. Practice using "I" statements and statements using a student's name in a respectful way aloud. The more you hear yourself say it, the more likely you are to do this naturally.

   _____

   _____

   _____

   _____

   _____

BEST PRACTICE #5

Create Purposeful Seating Charts

A big part of classroom management is giving every student opportunities to succeed. Have you ever seen a class that is doing a word search? Do you ever wonder why they drop down to almost silent immediately? **It's because they all can do the task.** The problem is that the task is too easy. Often, misbehaviors occur because students are underchallenged or over-challenged without academic support. This is where the tool of a purposeful seating chart can and will help your classroom management and improve the academic abilities of the class. With a purposeful seating chart, even with a challenging curriculum, students will always be in close proximity to those who can help them.

My mentor taught me a strategy for making seating charts that changed my teaching career. Before I learned this strategy, I used to break up students who "shouldn't sit together" and then sprinkle the rest around and hope for the best. This isn't the way to go. Making a purposeful seating chart means you look at students' academic abilities, learning disabilities, language barriers, and then make a chart from there. **I suggest having a seating chart done by Day 3 of the first week of school.** The earlier the better, or students will start finding who they want to sit next to, and then you'll have an extra battle on your hands. On the first day, if you do a student-centered lesson, you'll have the opportunity to observe how the students interact with each other. You'll need these observations to make a purposeful seating chart.

Tips for Preparing a Purposeful Seating Chart

Step #1: Acquire a list of students with IEPs in your class. You can usually find this on your attendance roster. It's helpful to have a description of the disability, but sometimes IEPs trickle in later in the school year. Work with what you have in the beginning of the school year.

Step #2: Find the list with the students who are English language learners (ELLs). Usually you can acquire this list from the speech pathologist at your school or the school counselor. It's easiest to get this information on your attendance roster, so check there first.

Step #3: Acquire a list of students identified as GATE (gifted and talented), often found on your attendance list.

The rest of your students should be in general education.

Draw out how you want to arrange the desks in your rooms. I recommend seating students in groups of four to six. Research suggests this is best for larger projects (Teaching & Learning Transformation Center, n.d.), and it will leave space in your classroom for movement. Situate the groups so students' backs are not toward the front of the room. You will be talking to the whole class many times, and you do not want students to constantly have to flip their chairs around to listen to you.

Step #4: Place your **students with IEPs first.** *Spread them out.* Some students may have preferential seating in their IEP, meaning they are legally mandated to sit in the front, back, or side depending on their needs.

Step #5: *Spread out* your **students identified as ELLs.** I usually put these students next to vocal general education students who speak often in class. If the general education student speaks the ELL student's native language, even better. These students will usually be eager to help a struggling EL student when needed. This makes a difference. Spread out the AVID (Advancement Via Individual Determination) students you may have, if you have that data.

Step #6: *Spread out* your **students identified as GATE.**

[handwritten margin note: ieps, ells, & gifted students (purposeful seating)]

You don't want to have a seating chart with "IEP" and other words written all over it, but you want to be able identify these students when you are teaching. Perhaps use a different color highlighter to color their names, or put a dot by the names of students with IEPs, ELLs, and GATE students. This way, you can remember what types of learners you have in the class as you are teaching.

A carefully planned seating chart in a class might look something like this:

Figure 5.1 A coded seating chart is most effective if it is always visible to the teacher. Dedicate a special place on your desk, or on your clipboard, where it is always in plain sight as you are teaching.

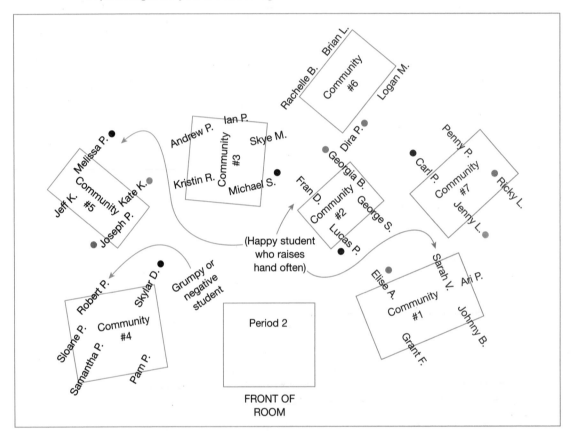

- student with IEP
- student identified as ELL (Keep in mind that advanced or early advanced ELLs may function quite similarly to general education students.)
- GATE student

You might want to put a code somewhere near your desk, but be careful about labeling student abilities right on the seating chart, as students will probably figure out who is who and feelings could be hurt. In addition, that is legally confidential information.

As you create your seating chart, you may also want to keep in mind these possible participants in your classroom:

One-on-One Adults in Your Room: If you have an adult who works one-on-one with a child, great! This student will be put in a group, and the adult will be in the group as another group member. It can be beneficial to put a "negative" student in this group, because the constant attention and proximity of another adult could turn a negative personality around, because this student won't have to fight for attention. It's worth a shot. I've seen it work. Just make sure the one-to-one adult and negative student aren't a personal clash, and the negative student isn't an explosive student. This isn't fair to anyone. It's a good idea to have a talk first with the other adult to let him know about the other students in the group, so he feels empowered to work with every student at their group.

Happy Students: I usually wait two days before making the seating chart to pick out the happy students who raise their hands often in the classroom. Happy students will reveal themselves fast, so usually I can spot them by Day 2. I try not to change seats after I make the seating chart on Day 3. I'll stick one dead center in the front and one dead center in the back. This keeps the class happy. See Best Practice #6 for more details on seating happy students.

Chronically Grumpy or Angry Students: Sometimes there are students who seem to have permanent black clouds over their heads. I can usually tell who these students are in the first few days. They make sly comments, they may exhibit outwardly defiant behaviors before the others, or they may just sit with their arms crossed your entire period. We want happy and vocal students eager to learn to become role models for these students, not the other way around. When identifying these students, you are looking for one trait: negativity. Most of the time, these students can be identified as quickly as the happy students.

As much as I'd like to wave a magic wand and have a smile appear on their faces, it's just not always possible. The fact is, the learning must go on. And we know that a grumpy or angry student doesn't learn as much as a happy student. Chronically grumpy and angry students need the most help, but their negative attitude shouldn't get most of your attention. If placed incorrectly, they may try to bring the class down with their negativity. With a properly made seating chart, we prevent this from happening. It's important that they are placed strategically. I'll usually set them on the side of the seating chart in front so they don't get lost in the back of the room or create a peanut gallery, and so their negative energy doesn't bleed into the class.

If you need to do a few seat swaps later, you can, the sooner the better, but make sure you still have the IEP, ELL, and GATE students evenly spread out among the general education students. In a perfect world, you wouldn't do any seat swaps, because consistency is the best in a classroom, but classrooms aren't always perfect and we're working with human beings. Most years I do one or two seat swaps in the first week and then leave the seating as is. The bottom line is that as teachers, we have to figure out a way to ensure that the whole class learns together. Once you make sure the learning of the class isn't hindered by a chronically grumpy or negative student, then you can go deeper into looking at the root causes of these emotions and help the student one on one.

Vocal Students: Make sure there's one vocal student at each community table. "Vocal" means a student that loves to share out. **I mark these students on my class roster Day 1 and 2 so I know to spread them out.** These are usually also the students who like to talk to their friends, too, and that's okay. Sometimes, the vocal students are the lowest-level ELL students, and I love when this happens. You want the student to be vocal (regardless of academic ability) because you want a focus of your class to be raising hands to answer and having a voice. It's fascinating how these students can encourage others to raise their hands as well. Use vocal students as resources to get strong participation from your classes. If each community group has someone raising a hand in the beginning, that will lead to others in the group following suit.

I then check the seating chart to make sure

1. Every low-level ELL is placed next to a general education student for academic support.

2. Two students with IEPs are not seated in the same group if possible.

This will give you a happy, mixed-ability class that has the most potential for success. Each student has a fighting chance to succeed. And—if you make a seating chart in the first week of class, you will learn student names much faster. It's a win-win.

In Figure 5.1, I placed the two hand-raising-happiest students in the center front and toward the center back, respectively, because **I want their energy to spread out to the class**. I then placed grumpy and/or angry students in Community #4. I now have a classroom where all students are given a chance to academically succeed. It's useful to keep this chart with you when you are teaching to check in on these students. If one table isn't grasping a concept, look at what learners you have at each table. Were three lower-level ELL students accidentally placed together? There are so many uses to having this type of seating chart. This is why my students don't choose their own seats.

There's a small chance that if you explain to anybody how you decided seats for your class, they may be offended because you're looking at cognitive abilities rather than other factors. But what you are actually doing is making the focus of your class academic success, collaboration, and engagement, and giving each student a chance to succeed based on the skills and knowledge they have. If you want to teach challenging curriculum, include student collaboration regularly in your lessons, and ensure that students are to be able to perform academically; this way works.

Changing It Up in High School

In high school, I have my students move their desks into different formations, depending on the learning plan that class period. Doing this once a week is usually enough to make this type of arrangement special, and it can really spice up a lesson. High school students can move desks around fast, so you need to have a bit more flexibility with changing the desks around to best fit the discussion needs of the lesson. The arrangement in your chart can be your "home base" arrangement.

In high school, depending on your discipline, you may want to rearrange seats in a way that fosters the **type of conversations** you have in the classroom.

- In a high school English classroom, if the space allows, a circle or horseshoe makes sense to have discussions about text in a seminar-type lesson.

- In a high school history class, a class divided down the center makes sense to debate two different sides of the story or historical event.

- In a high school math class, groups make sense to foster working collaboratively in teams to solve math problems.

- In a high school science class, groups make the most sense to complete labs.

In each of these seating arrangements, students of different cognitive levels should be spread out.

You could also use this type of dynamic seating style the second half of the year in an upper-grade middle school classroom. They may just need more help arranging the desks (maybe project a visual of what each shape looks like when you ask them to move the desks), and leave a few more minutes to get the desks back to their original positions at the end of the class.

Changing It Up in Elementary and Middle School

If you'd like to try different formations in elementary and middle school, you can, but if you have any sort of behavior modification or rewards system with your community groups, it will be hard to reward groups the day you do a different seating arrangement. If you do not have a behavior modification system or classwide reward system with your groups, just make sure you don't change the arrangement so often that students forget where their home base seats are. So, I'd do it sparingly in the middle school grades—perhaps maybe once per unit during a debate, Socratic seminar, or other special activity.

Flexible Seating

Flexible seating means that students choose their own seats based on where they feel most comfortable and/or learn best. Also, in flexible seating, students often have unique seating arrangements such as bean bags, the carpeted floor, or swivel stools. Although flex seating has certain benefits and is often preferred by students, I don't recommend using this arrangement in your first years. Here are a few reasons why:

Something to keep in mind with this is that students are unaware of their classmates' special classifications (if any), meaning students do not know each other's ELL levels, or which students have IEPs or are classified as gifted and talented. Flexible seating should still provide students with opportunities for collaboration. It can disrupt a full-class behavior modification program based on groups or communities, because students maybe constantly changing their seats. Also, with flexible seating, self-chosen student groups will likely be academically uneven in skill level, compared to one another. I usually had classrooms with a high percentage of ELLs, as well as a high percentage of students with IEPs. Therefore I found that my seating chart worked best to scaffold instruction and create a positive learning environment, which is crucial to learning. My students needed to collaborate and needed to be grouped based on varying abilities to understand the material. When I allowed flexible seating, usually the students with low ELL levels grouped together, the students with high academic ability grouped together, and so on. Learners tend to naturally gravitate to people like them. Remember, students may be so exited to be able to have flexible seating that they agree to be more focused. However, we know that a quiet classroom does not always mean that students are learning the most or grappling with the material. Remember the word search example from the beginning of this section? It's a fine balance.

Tips for Flexible Seating

If you are curious about trying flexible seating, I suggest you

1. Use the seating arrangement proposed in the tips at the beginning of this section as the students' home base or normal seating. The home base seats usually work best for instruction time.

2. Try it out in small bits: Perhaps try flexible seating mildly at first, meaning, if students are working in table groups, you could let the group choose where they want to sit in the room during work time. The groups should stay together. For example, during groupwork time, one group may go to the carpet together and sit in a circle if that works for them and they are more comfortable.

3. Use it at first with a class that needs less academic or language scaffolding, for example, a class with mostly GATE or general education students. The seating arrangement provided provides solid academic support. So, students who need less academic support might do better with flexible seating.

4. Have a lesson teaching students how to pick the seat best for them.

5. Try it out with just one class first.

Tips for Making a Seating Chart

1. Print out a class roster before Day 1 of the school year.

2. During class, mark
    a. happy, engaged students
    b. grumpy, angry students
    c. vocal students

    Use just one letter or codes so students can't interpret.

3. Keep an eye on the same students for Day 2. Are they marked accurately?

4. Before Day 3, print out your list of students with IEPs, ELL students, and GATE students. (This information usually can be found on your attendance list if you look closely.)

5. Arrange the desks the way you'd like first, before Day 3.

6. Draw a seating chart for each class. First, place your students with IEPs and those identified as ELLs based on where they will learn best. Next, place GATE students. Then, place your happy students definitely first, toward the center and then spread out evenly. Then, place your negative students on the side where they have room and aren't physically accidentally bumped often. These students usually like space.

7. Spread out the general education students in the remaining seats.

8. Color code your chart based on type of student so you have a reference during class to check for understanding. Be as discreet as possible when making the color code legend on the seating chart. Assume a student will see it at some point during the year, and shouldn't be able to understand the legend. This step is very important also if you have to switch students between seats (that usually happens); you can make sure they switch to where they will still balance out a table academically.

Your turn

1. What are your thoughts on the heterogeneous seating chart and spreading out the students with IEPs, general education students, ELL students, et cetera?

   _____

   _____

   _____

2. How would you do small group instruction in your room? Do you have a designated area?

   _____

   _____

   _____

3. What are your thoughts on spreading out happy engaged students and also spreading out negative students? Do you think this has benefit to a classroom?

   _____

   _____

   _____

4. Do you have another way you would like to do a seating chart? Talk to your coteacher or another colleague about this and gather some ideas. (Remember: If you want the focus of the class to be on academics and engagement, then you have to look at these criteria—that is, "the data"—first when arranging students.)

   _____

   _____

   _____

Real Conversation With Eighth-Grade Student

Student: Ms. Pariser, what do you call pasta that is not real?

Me: I don't know.

Student: An impasta!

Me: [laughs loudly]

Student [to another student]:   See, that's how you know they are getting old, when they laugh at that.

Student [to me]:   It was just a social experiment.

PART 2

FORMING POSITIVE RELATIONSHIPS WITH YOUR STUDENTS

What Doesn't Help Form a Positive Relationship With a Student

My eighth-grade English teacher put a very talkative boy in the closet to get him to stop talking, and forgot about him. The boy went to sleep and woke at 6:00 p.m. when he heard the janitor cleaning the room.

—Ellen, age 69

Image Credit: Mia Regala www.paper-scraps.com

How does forming positive relationships with your students relate to classroom management?

Connection is the strongest form of classroom management, but it's virtually impossible to have a strong connection with every one of your students. There just aren't enough hours in the day. In a realistic sense, positive relationships lead to a more pleasant classroom environment all year long and a more powerful learning and teaching experience for you and the students. Investing in building positive relationships with students means understanding off-task behavior and knowing how to intervene appropriately to empower students. It means generally they will be excited to come to your class and look forward to seeing *you* every day. Some days they may not, and that's okay but don't take it personally. It's usually not personal.

I REMEMBER WHEN. . . .

I remember my first day of finally having my own classroom. I was both nervous and excited. It was March and I was taking over a first-grade class for a teacher who had moved out of state. When I was walking to pick up the class, a parent came up to me and asked, "Are you the new teacher in Room 3?"

"Yes, I am!"

She proceeded to tell me that her son Fred was in my class and that I was not to let him get away with anything. She told me that I had to be strict with Fred or he would become a big behavior issue for me. This parent was very loud and demanding, and I was honestly intimidated by her. So instead of doing what I felt was right, I listened to her. I spoke to Fred differently than I spoke to the rest of the class. I asked other kids nicely to do things, but with Fred I used my firm, "I mean business" teacher voice. I gave Fred timeouts, he missed recess, and I didn't let him get away with anything, just like his mom had requested.

But the problem was, Fred, in turn, didn't like me. His behavior actually got worse, and what I was doing obviously wasn't working. I nervously called Fred's mother in for a meeting and told her I had tried her way and it just did not fit with my personality. I suggested that we try positive means to change Fred's behavior. I started using sticker charts, tickets, rewards, and most of all just complimenting Fred on the things he was doing right. She was very adamant that those things would never work with Fred, but she agreed to let me try. It didn't happen overnight, but Fred's behavior began to turn around. He realized that I liked him and cared about him and began to try. You know the saying, "You'll get more with sugar than with salt?" Well it's true, and I learned it first-hand with Fred.

—Erika Perez
21 years' experience
Jefferson Elementary IB
STEAM Magnet School
San Diego, California

BEST PRACTICE #6

Use Your Power for Good, Not Evil

. . . .

> You can tell when a teacher trusts you because they listen to you.
> I actually do more work in their classes because I know they want
> me to succeed.
>
> —Penny, Grade 9

There's a quote that used to hang in the back of my private teacher cabinet. I printed it out in twelve-point type, large enough for me to read but small enough for a student not to see if he or she accidentally opened up the cabinet (which sometimes happened).

"A teacher holds the power to single-handedly change the atmosphere of a classroom."

I felt as if I had discovered the secret to life. *That's a lot of power to have!* I thought to myself. I would be lying if I told you that I utilized that quote every single day after, but it still is in my thoughts constantly today. I follow this credo. We teachers are the **emotional leaders** in the classroom.

Think of a presentation you have had to sit through. Audience members or students tend to take on the energy of the presenter. Have you ever felt energized after a presentation because the lead presenter was smiling, stimulating, and thought-provoking? Now think of the opposite. Have you ever felt drained after listening to a monotonous, long-winded, and boring presenter? We have the power to control the mood of the class. My goal is usually to make the students smile and laugh in the beginning of class.

Don't be afraid of not being able to get their attention back. I believe this is what stops some educators from letting the class start with inspiration rather than intimidation.

stay positive!

When I taught middle school in my first few years, I spent the first five or ten minutes of class asking Shannon to stop fidgeting or Mark to stop banging on the desk. By the time I started the lesson, I was already frustrated and exhausted! Pretty soon I changed tactics. Instead, before I started each lesson, I tried to remember to glance at a simple reminder I had pasted to my teacher station to remind me that my mood and my energy will radiate to the class. My reminder was a tiny strip of paper that said one word: POSITIVE. I placed it where I would see it many times throughout the lesson. That tiny strip of paper helped many days when I needed the reminder for the sake of the class. We all need our reminders from time to time. I knew if I could be positive, even if I felt differently inside some days, learning would be ten thousand times easier for them. Sometimes in my smaller classes I would tell a joke, often the ones on the Laffy Taffy wrappers or something simple I picked up somewhere. For example, after all of our serious work was finished and we had a minute or two left in the class, I would sometimes say,

Me:	Okay, we have an extra minute left of class and I have some new material.
Class [whining]:	Oh Ms. Pariser, not again! [smiling]
Me:	How do you make a tissue dance? Anyone? Anyone?
Class:	[scream out various answers]
Me:	[screaming back with excitement] *Put a little boogie in it!*

Some students would look disgusted and some would laugh, but either way the sound of laughter was in the classroom. In ten seconds, I got half the class laughing. They were becoming conditioned to the positive vibe and associating that feeling with our classroom. I was always careful to learn for which classes this would work, and it was often the smaller classes.

Easier said than done, right? Making the toughest inner-city students smile before you start teaching them is one example of using your power for good. On any given day, we could spend the first five or ten minutes, or even the whole period, focusing on the negative. It's just easier to do. "Johnny, why don't you have a pencil?" "Suzy, turn around." Before you know it you'll have ten more behavior problems that you didn't have before. Why? Where was your attention? That's where the students will focus as well. I've always thought the positive was so much harder to focus on, but worth it. Isn't that true in life?

Tips for Focusing on the Positive

1. Praise the positive from the moment they step into your room.

A person who feels appreciated will always do more than expected.

—Amy Rees Anderson

I spend the first three to four minutes of each period solely on positively reinforcing specific student behavior, saying things such as, "Julie, *thank you* for getting started silently on the board work." What happens when I say this? Other students scramble to take out their planners. They want recognition, and everybody loves to be appreciated. Or I'll say, "I *really appreciate* how everyone at Table 3 is sitting down. I like how Christine's table is about to refocus." What happens? Students scramble to sit down. Christine's table agrees and refocuses. It's a self-fulfilling statement. The trick is to never to be condescending or sarcastic. Be genuine.

Think about this: If a teacher were to say, "Orman, can't you see how Table 3 is all sitting? Why can't you do that?" this teacher would be trying to reach the same goal (seated students) that I'm reaching for, right? But not only did this teacher embarrass Orman, she also set a negative tone in the classroom and set herself up for failure for that lesson—with everyone. Who wants to teach or learn in that kind of environment? The same positive dialogue can be used with grade school or tough high school students successfully. Nobody is too old to get positive attention, even ourselves.

We all want the same things: love, attention, and feeling we belong. The funny thing about this trick is that you have to be specific in what you praise. Think of what you'd like your class to do, and then praise the individuals who are doing it. It works. Two years ago I decided I wanted students to clap for each other. It made the learning different, more supportive, and fun. I started the next year by saying, "That was a beautiful answer; it would have been so nice if somebody had clapped." Low and behold, somebody did clap for the next answer—as a joke, but the students were still smiling. Before the end of the period, after I constantly praised that specific clapping behavior, high school students—yes, high school students—were all clapping for each other when they answered. That may be a little too much for you, but perhaps not. You'd be surprised how fun it can make learning.

2. Know that the mind is more open when it is happy.

The most successful companies know this. Google lets their employees bring their dogs to work and has pool tables in the break room (Steward, 2013). This successful company knows that when the mind is happy, innovation flows. Think of how you feel when you are scared, sad, or angry. Are you open to learn? Now think of how your mind feels when you are peaceful and comfortable. The mind is a sponge. Yes, students will be quieter if you yell, but I always think of it as their mind's doors slamming shut. Keep your tone gentle; talk **to** the students and not at them. Talking to the students means you are talking to connect with them. Talking **at** a student means you are talking to silence them. This is sometimes more difficult to do in a larger classroom, where you have to make sure everybody hears you. Keep your mind always on the goal: The students must learn. You want to keep their minds open. A happy student is a good producer of quality thinking and work.

Once a positive classroom environment is established, it can continue throughout the school year. The students will become conditioned to having a positive attitude. Sometimes school is the only place a student will receive praise! You will be the parent they do not have. If the class does slip into a negative tone for a few days, all you have to do is bring it back to the question, *How do we get our positive classroom back?* Perhaps you brainstorm with your class, or perhaps you use your own ideas. Usually, it's just a few key small adjustments, because the students already are confident that they know how to be positive. However, once a class crosses to what I call "the point of little or no return," it takes one heck of a teacher to get them back, but it is doable.

3. Set a few happy students in the center of the classroom.

Every class has a different personality. The students take on energy. In the beginning of the year, before its personality has surfaced yet, the class will typically follow the student who appears to be a leader. Any group of people looks for a leader. You actually can decide which student you want to lead the class. You want the students who smile, respect and help others with their words and actions, and eagerly raise their hands to become the natural leaders in each class. You can make this happen.

I learned this trick—focusing on the positive—one year when I could not figure out why my one class had suddenly switched from happy to grumpy, moody, and overall blah. There was one particular girl whom I had recently switched to the center of the room when it all started. I switched her seat because she was talking too much to her friend on the side of the room. She wore heavy black eyeliner, and her mood seemed to match her dark makeup every day. I felt like she was not getting enough attention, so I put her right in front of me. Big mistake. My life as a teacher became very difficult for the next few weeks, until I figured out what was going on. She had a presence and demeanor that other students watched and emulated. Students, like any other people—or animals for that matter—tend to mimic what they see.

Soon, I had students to her left talking back. *What the heck?!?* I thought. How is she telegraphing her negative attitude? Ahh! It all clicked! Just as you have the power to spread your mood all around the classroom, so do the students in the center of the room.

Now, do not make the mistake of sitting all of the positive students in the center. You'll have a heck of a time trying to control the other areas. Just sit two or three students who raise their hands and are smiley in the center, and you'll be surprised how their energy will create a positive mood for your whole classroom. See Best Practice #5 for how to seat the happy and engaged students and also the grumpy students. A smile is contagious and it just works!

Remember:

▶ You are the emotional leader of the classroom.

▶ Your energy will radiate out into the classroom.

▶ If needed, keep a visual reminder somewhere where you will see it often.

▶ What you focus on will thrive in the classroom.

▶ Do not seat negative students in the center of your classroom.

Your turn

1. What behaviors or habits do you want to see more of in your classroom? Have you been praising the student who demonstrates these behaviors genuinely? Ask yourself when you can praise these specific habits or behaviors in class. You may need to write yourself a reminder to use during the first few weeks, and either post it on your desk or slip it into your lesson plans.

_____

_____

_____

_____

_____

_____

_____

2. How can you make your students happy? Can you use one of your strengths for this? List three things you can do or say in the near future to put a smile on your students' faces.

_____

_____

_____

_____

_____

_____

_____

Let Students Make Mistakes Without Feeling Like Failures

I used to spend the first week of school making sure the kids were quiet and obedient, and knew my rules. I now spend a little bit of time on rules, but mainly I teach the students how to **get over their fear of making mistakes** when sharing or presenting. Students come to me each year with the notion that quieter is better than talking and making a mistake. This frustrates me year after year. By Week 2, my students usually understand that I want to hear their voices, that I need to hear what they have learned so that I can reguide them if necessary. I don't get angry or frustrated with a wrong answer. It is just one step closer to the right answer. Let's look at some examples of how to redirect students without making them feel stupid or embarrassed in front of their peers.

Scenario A

Teacher: What do you think is the theme of this story?

Student 1:   Animals?

Teacher: Really? Really? After three theme lessons you think the theme is animals? Have you been paying attention? That's wrong.

I would assume there would have to be a lot of teacher wait time after this response, because the teacher's response makes students afraid to share unless they are certain they are right. This means the teacher can really only tell what a few of the students are thinking. Let's look at the same example from another teacher.

Scenario B

Teacher: What do you think is the theme of this story?

Student 1:   Animals?

Teacher: Okay, I see where you're going, who can help her out a bit?

Student 2:   Well, it's about animals but more about humans, too.

Teacher: Okay, we have good stuff here to work with. So now, what do you guys think the theme is? Remember what theme means?

Student 3:   Man Versus Nature!

Teacher: Exactly.

It's really hard to unlearn failure. When kids get the idea in their head that they failed at something, it stays with them. Be somebody in their life who shows them mistakes are part of growth. It takes an extreme amount of patience and practice to do this, but is well worth the payoff. Who doesn't want a classroom of students who aren't afraid to answer?

IN A SAFE MISTAKE-MAKING ENVIRONMENT	IN AN UNSAFE MISTAKE-MAKING ENVIRONMENT
Teacher uses "incorrect" answers to guide class to the "correct" answers.	Teacher says, "No, that's wrong."
Students know not to shame each other for giving a wrong answer.	Students in class laugh or ridicule when a student gives a wrong answer.
Many hands are raised for each question asked. Students are eager to try.	Students are afraid to raise their hands.
Teacher asks classmates to "help out" when an incorrect answer is shared.	Teacher gets frustrated easily when an incorrect answer is shared.

Your turn

1. Were you ever in a class where you felt safe making a mistake? How did the teacher or instructor create this environment?

_____

_____

_____

2. How did this maximize the learning for you and the other students? Why did you feel more comfortable raising your hand to share?

_____

_____

_____

3. Now answer the questions above for a class you remember where you were fearful of making a mistake.

_____

_____

_____

4. What type of classroom do you want? With a partner, practice your responses as a teacher when a student makes a mistake. Ask your partner how he felt when you responded this way.

_____

_____

_____

BEST PRACTICE #8

Win Over the Tough Kids

It sucks when teachers don't trust me. It makes me question if they think I'm a good person.

—Jocelyn, Grade 9

There isn't a teacher alive who hasn't dealt with a tough student. I remember my first year. I thought administration was playing a joke on me when I was handed my roster. "There are no good kids in my class!" I thought. Why would they give the most inexperienced teacher in the school all the rough kids? Were they trying to weed me out? How am I supposed to use anything I learned in any of my college classes with this group?

There was one student in particular, "Dennis." He looked a little older than the other sixth graders. He watched me for a few weeks before he started acting up. It was like he was more confident and aggressive than the others. Each day he had a little more attitude than the day before. I didn't understand because the neighboring teacher did not have the same issues as I with this student. I remember a specific day when Dennis had a basketball in his hand as he lined up for my class. He bounced it and looked at me.

Me: Don't bounce that ball or I'll take it.

Dennis: [smiles] [bounces ball]

I walk over, reach to take the basketball and he gracefully swoops it behind his back. The kid had skills. Now, I've dug my own hole. I can't reach for it anymore without really jeopardizing my job, and he has won the battle. I retreat, fuming, and he bounces it again. The other kids laugh. Now I am supposed to start my lesson? Really?

Thankfully, this doesn't happen anymore. There's a way to not get yourself in this situation. We've all learned, some like myself the hard way.

First of all, with the tough kids, they are used to being disciplined and scolded, not valued or even liked. This is sadly what they are comfortable with. Do you want to be the same as every other teacher, or do you want to be kinder and more respectful than the others? They'll respect you more for the latter if you still stay firm with your classroom structure.

The bottom line is that the tough kids want to be treated like everybody else. They want to be spoken to like everyone else; they want to be considered as smart as everyone else. Why don't they act like everyone else? This is where you have to be the adult and start the learning process of how to connect with them. First, treat them like every other student. That will answer ninety-nine percent of all of your questions about them. Students misbehave for one of four reasons (or a mesh of different reasons):

1. They want power.
2. They feel inadequate.
3. They want to get even.
4. They want attention that they are not getting elsewhere. (Walker, 2014)

If you can pinpoint the main reason, you can find a solution that works. Remember, **they don't know why they are misbehaving**; they just do sometimes. It's our job to figure it out and help them become successful. Let's run back through the same scenario. First of all, I challenged Dennis from the beginning. I challenged his reputation in front of the class. Of course he wasn't going to back down and stop bouncing the ball. Here's how I may handle this situation today, if Dennis were bouncing the ball as class was lining up:

Me: Hey Dennis, I didn't know you played basketball. Are you on the team?

Dennis: No.

Me: Do me a favor please (always have the students do "you" a favor—the wording just works) and let's hold off and not bounce the ball right now. I really appreciate it. I don't mind holding the ball for you if it makes it easier.

Speak to students with this much respect. That is how I speak to my students now, as do most other successful teachers. Some use their "teacher power" more than others, but I always think you should approach that method with caution.

Most of the time, students will oblige if you respect them, set your boundaries (you let him know bouncing a ball is not acceptable at this time), and are willing to meet them half way (willing to hold it for him). At no time would this student have felt threatened or demeaned, but you achieve the same or better results. Try not to use your teacher power if you do not have to. Teacher power should be saved for those special situations where it would be most useful. Yes, it's easier and quicker at times, but the repercussions are severe and this tactic rarely works with the tough kids. They aren't used to being respected and might very well act differently for you if you treat them differently than other teachers have in the past.

My beliefs about children's behavior have changed over the years. I no longer believe there are any "bad" kids as I did my first year. I referred to the tougher kids with this phrase because I was frustrated that I could not get through to them. I later found that these students were the ones who shaped my teaching career. They were the ones who challenged me, the ones I worked the hardest for, the ones that touched my heart, and the ones who came back years later to visit. These are the students who make or break teachers.

More Tips for Teaching Tough Students

- Give them their space when they need it.

- Find at least one quality you like about them.

- Find out one thing outside of school they are interested in. If a student likes cars, pick up a car magazine and let them know you thought they might be interested in it. If they like skateboarding, ask them to bring in a picture of them skating and tell them you'd love to hang it in the classroom to show off their skills. Show them you care about them.

- Don't take students' misbehaviors personally. It's usually not about us. This can be very difficult for us to do. Realize this. They are going through something and they are children, or teenagers.

- Do not hold a grudge. Start every day optimistic about their behavior.

- Find their strengths and let them use their strengths in the classroom. If you don't, sometimes a strength can also cause the most trouble in the classroom. Think of the student who is a wonderful articulator, but is always silenced. That student will find a time to talk, whether you give it to him or not. Give him room to shine.

- Don't make everything a fight. Ask individual students to do what you want them to do quietly and privately; don't demand they do it publically. They need to save face in front of the class. Otherwise, they will challenge you. Do you want to take on this unneeded fight or power struggle?

Your turn

1. When was the last time you used your "teacher power" in your classroom? Was it necessary or not? Why?

_____

_____

_____

_____

2. Think of the toughest student in each of your classes. What is this student interested in? How can you find this out?

_____

_____

_____

_____

3. Think of the toughest student in each of your classes. What are this student's academic strengths? How can you use this to help the class?

_____

_____

_____

_____

Become a Teacher Detective

When a student doesn't do work in your class, **it's usually not personal.** However, it can feel personal to us, since we put countless hours into our lesson planning. Let me break it down for you. I spent a few months frustrated that my students never had organized binders. They had papers spilling out of the sides and out of order. Our school policy was that each classroom teacher had to make sure students had binders organized. The first time I asked students to take out their binders, I almost had a heart attack. "What? This is what you consider clean?!?" I yelled, I scolded, I threatened detention, and still the binders remained messy.

This was about the same time I was getting my master's degree in educational technology at San Diego State University, and we studied a concept that I will explain in this section. Suddenly, it clicked. They just needed time. Teachers were giving them papers at rocket speed and not giving them time in class to put the papers in the correct sections. They knew how to clean out the binders, and they wanted to have cleaner binders, they just were not given time to do the organizing. It was such a simple concept and answer: They needed time. We all have these moments in teaching where a simple solution takes longer than needed to discover. Let me speed up the process for you to save some time.

I've come to believe that laziness explains why students do not work only 33.3 percent of the time. There are actually two other reasons. In my master's classes, we used a text, _Analyzing Performance Problems,_ by Robert Mager and Peter Pipe (1997) that discussed a few reasons why people don't perform when asked; these are known as _performance problems_. Basically, it states that there are a few (it's really that simple) reasons that a human being will not do something. In the classroom we can almost always narrow it down to one of three barriers that prevent students from performing. Ready? Drum roll please. The three reasons are these:

1. **Skills/Knowledge:** If skills/knowledge is the performance barrier, the student does not have the skill or knowledge to complete the task. A learning disability may be this type of barrier, such as a reading disability or a processing disability. In this case, the teacher can either reteach the material in a mini lesson or tutoring session, or pair the student with a more knowledgeable peer for a specific task. Or, perhaps the work was just too difficult. For example, if a student who really wanted to earn an A on a paper did not know how to compose a proper concluding paragraph, she would be lacking the necessary skills and knowledge to be successful. She would need a refresher or full lesson on how to compose the paper.

2. **Motivation:** If motivation is the performance barrier, the student does not have a reason motivating enough to do the work or task. As teachers, we can easily mistake this performance barrier for laziness. However, the formula for motivation is value times confidence. Think: $V \times C$. So, if one of the variables is 0, the product is zero. Students have to find value in what they are doing and know they can do it, even if it takes some help. Value can be defined as seeing something as important or "mattering," for whatever reason. This can be for many different reasons. For example, a student who wants to play in the soccer game after school knows he needs to complete the assignment to do so. The student sees the assignment as mattering for this reason. Or, a student could see value in a Spanish assignment because she wants to take AP Spanish next year and knows that she needs to learn her verbs to do so. Both of these students have motivating factors that add value to an assignment for that student.

   In this case, the teacher could assign a grade, add on a competitive factor to the project, or speak to the class about the purpose of the task. Hint: It's always easier to use extrinsic motivation to get students motivated, but intrinsic motivation is a thousand times more powerful. Extrinsic motivation often leads to intrinsic motivation. Think of extrinsic motivation as training wheels to help students find intrinsic motivation.

   Extrinsic motivation can sometimes be a barrier. For example, a student might know how to compose a paper but just not care to finish it, because good grades are not a driving motivator, or the student might not need the grade for some reason. As educators, especially middle and high school teachers, we have to remember that students have many things going on in their nonacademic lives. Get them to want to please you. Sometimes we are a parent substitute. Our job is to teach them how to balance these factors (significant others, family drama, friend drama) to stay motivated in school.

> It is always easier to use extrinsic motivation to get students motivated, but intrinsic motivation is a thousand times more powerful.

3. **Resources:** If lack of resources is the performance barrier, the student does not have the time or resources to do the work or task.

   Basically, students either do not know how to do a task, do not have a reason valuable enough to do it (intrinsic or extrinsic), or do not have the time or materials to do it. It can also be a combination of two or three, but there is usually one driving force.

Wow. Really? This is it. With this knowledge, as a teacher, you can usually "fix" the problem and get students back to work. Many times they will not understand why they are not working, or be able to articulate their needs, but you can now use this information to correctly diagnose the issue. Okay, let's look at an example:

Scenario #1: "Lazy" Guillermo

Guillermo is sitting at his desk with a paper in front of him and not working. He has a pencil in his hand and seemed to understand the lesson when the teacher was teaching, but still is not working. The teacher goes over and says if he does not start working, he will have to stay after school. Guillermo gets angry and says he cannot stay after school and hates this stupid project. The teacher calls home, the project does not get completed, and Guillermo and the teacher are angry with each other.

Okay, take a breath. Now, let's look at this scenario from another standpoint.

Scenario #2: "Lazy" Guillermo (a closer look)

Guillermo is sitting at his desk with a paper in front of him and not working. He has a pencil in his hand and seemed to understand the lesson when the teacher was teaching, but still is not working. The teacher goes over and asks what he needs. Guillermo says he doesn't know. The teacher asks if he needs help getting started. Guillermo says maybe. The teacher and Guillermo come up with the answer to the first question together. Guillermo smiles and after two more problems, can do the rest on his own.

It is not always this picture perfect, but you get the idea. What was the difference between the two scenarios? The teacher did the detective work. Here's what went on in her head: "I know the barrier is not motivation because Guillermo really wants the grade; I know he has a pencil, time, and paper to work; so it must be skills/knowledge. I wonder if he just needs a little help." Also, in the first example, the teacher angered Guillermo. An angry student will almost never ask for help.

If you want to take it one step further, this theory can be applied anywhere (even with colleagues). Next time you hear your not-so-pleasant-at-6:00-a.m.-on-no-coffee colleague say, "Why can't I learn to use this copy machine!" you can now ask yourself, *Is this colleague not performing because of a lack of skills/ knowledge (the colleague just does not know how to work the thousand buttons), motivation (there is no reason to learn), or resources (there is not any paper, or the colleague doesn't have time to learn)?* You will be surprised how this problem-solving thinking can change your career into being a teacher detective. Be careful about sharing this knowledge with other adults; it can seem a little pretentious if you do not vent with them about how nothing is fixable. Sometimes people just want and need to vent, and you can just listen. However, use this information in your classroom and see the results!

Why do students work for some teachers and not as much for others? The teachers they work for have tapped into performance barrier thinking, perhaps on a subconscious level. If they know this information to some extent, they will make sure the students have the time and materials to work, know how to teach the content so the students understand it (skills/knowledge), and know how to motivate students with either (or both) extrinsic or intrinsic motivation in their classrooms.

So are students lazy? Perhaps sometimes, but now you know that it is only because they are not either intrinsically or extrinsically motivated for some reason. Be the detective. Figure out how to fix it, or at least start with having compassion. Students rarely can diagnose themselves. Add an element of competition, use grades as a factor, and/or explain the purpose of the assignment (and it better be meaningful).

Now, you hold this power. Use it wisely and see the results. I found in my years of teaching that figuring out how to eliminate the barriers that prevented students from putting energy into their work was exhilarating.

PERFORMANCE BARRIER	WHAT DOES IT LOOK LIKE IN THE CLASSROOM?	STRATEGIES FOR INTERVENTION
Resources	Student "frozen" and not working but not asking for help	Privately ask student what he needs to begin
		Reach out to parents to make sure student has necessary materials for class
	Student overly talkative during work time	Privately ask student how much sleep she is getting at night and if she is eating breakfast
	Student sleeping during class time	Have a one-to-one student conference
		Introduce a system where students can check out paper, pencils, other needed supplies in your classroom
		Give a mini lesson on time management

PERFORMANCE BARRIER	WHAT DOES IT LOOK LIKE IN THE CLASSROOM?	STRATEGIES FOR INTERVENTION
Skills/Knowledge	Student "frozen" and not working but not asking for help Student overly talkative during work time Students not participating in lesson	Pull student into small group instruction with an adult in the room Ask your coteacher to reteach the concept in a different way in a mini lesson Reteach the concept in a mini lesson Have students reteach each other difficult concepts in small, student-led groups Have student lead a small group of struggling students in reteaching concept If student has an IEP, and the lack of skills/knowledge is hindering the student from succeeding in your class, contact the case manager or school psychologist for strategies to work with student academically Sign student up for tutoring Increase collaboration in your lessons Increase informal "checks for understanding" in your lessons
Motivation (value × confidence) neither variable can be zero	Student "frozen" and not working but not raising hand Student overly talkative during work time Student sleeping during class time Student has difficulty concentrating, lacks engagement	Add a competitive aspect to the lesson, unit, or project (value) Let students know you believe in their success (confidence) Ask students to praise each other after a day of group work (confidence) Praise student for participating (confidence) Create a behavior/work contract for student if consistent issue (value) Use a behavior modification system for the whole class (value) Have a one-on-one conference with student to build confidence in task (confidence) Reach out to parent about student's lack of motivation (value) Explain to student privately how assignment fits into bigger picture (value) Update students regularly on their current class grades (value) Try project- or problem-based unit in your classroom (value)

Note: There can be more than one barrier, but the key is to find the barrier that is keeping that student from working the most and intervene accordingly.

Your turn

1. Think of a student who never seems motivated. Now, with the new knowledge you have from reading about this best practice, determine whether motivation is this student's biggest barrier to performance, or whether it is one of the other two. Remember that it can be a mixture of a few, but usually one is the biggest. Target the biggest, and use the table to help you brainstorm ways to give the student the support needed to overcome it.

    _____

    _____

    _____

2. Based on what you learned about performance problems, what does this student need the most to be successful based on the biggest barrier? What actions do you need to take to make this happen?

    _____

    _____

    _____

    _____

3. Do the same with another student that you previously considered or others misdiagnosed. What different steps might you need to take to help this student?

    _____

    _____

    _____

    _____

BEST PRACTICE #10

Spread Positivity with Your Words and Tone

This is the happiest family ever!

—Emily, Grade 8 [describing her
English classroom experience]

This section is short but one of the most important. When teachers speak to a class, they are giving off energy, a vibe. Next time you listen to someone speak, listen to the tone of his voice rather than what he is saying. Is he giving off a positive energy, or negative, sad, disappointed, or even threatening energy? I always try to use my vocal power to add positive energy to the room. We don't all have to be cheerleaders, but you can show you care with the words you use and your tone. When I hear negative teachers speak to a class, it is draining for the students. I know this because it drains me. I never understood how students are supposed to learn in that environment. Do you drain or do you inspire?

Second, listen to how loudly you speak to a student. The trick is to **mimic the volume you desire from them**.

- If you speak *too loudly* you will silence a class. They most likely will either get very quiet, or get really loud to try to overpower your voice.

- If you speak *too quietly*, they just won't pay attention because they won't hear you.

▶ If you speak *gently, but firmly* with a moderate volume, they will mimic you, and you will have an effective environment for learning. They will naturally meet your energy and voice level.

Ideas on how to gauge your voice and tone:

▶ Record a part of your lesson one day on your phone, and listen to the recording. How did your volume and tone make you feel? Keep doing this until you find the right balance.

▶ Ask your coteacher in the classroom about your tone specifically.

▶ Video-record yourself teaching a lesson, and watch the video to listen for your tone and volume.

Your turn

1. Think of a favorite teacher you've had in your lifetime. How was his tone and volume when he spoke? How did it make you feel?

    _____

    _____

    _____

    _____

2. How do you want your students to feel in your classroom?

    _____

    _____

    _____

    _____

3. How do you think your "teacher voice" makes students feel? In your opinion, do you need to improve your tone or not? Why?

    _____

    _____

    _____

    _____

Focus on the Positive and Create Positive Students

The first two weeks of any school year are wonderful. Everything is fresh, your classroom is spotless, you stay on top of your workload, and you have the one stack of papers from your first assignment graded. All of the students are quieter in the classroom because they do not know each other fully yet, and the students are eagerly waiting for your next lesson.

Around the third week of school, something interesting usually happens. A few students in the class test your limits. Don't worry; they will test gently at first. This is the nature of human beings. We all do it. Students are not any different. The third week of school will test your patience, most likely. The key to this week and weeks following is to focus on the positive. Beware if you focus on the students who are testing the rules. These students should be given the consequences you have put in place, privately if possible. But overall, keep the energy in the room positive.

One of the most powerful ways to keep the vibe of the classroom positive is with your words and demeanor. Always look as if you are in control, smile, and keep the pacing going! Would an actor stop a show for one distraction? Probably not. An amateur actor might. See the comparison? Have your consequences set in place (Week 1 works the best to set your class expectations and clear consequences), follow through, and use them when needed as a tool, not a weapon. Assign the consequences quickly and privately, and use

"I" statements. Be calm, not angry. Stay in control. The teaching and momentum are more important.

Here are two different ways to speak to the class on Week 3:

Positive Ms. Patterson:	I just love how quietly you came into the room. You really know how to follow directions. Almost all of you have your books out and are ready to read. Once the last two students get their books out, we'll be ready. I'm amazed, class!

OR

Negative Mr. Netherland:	You came into the room all right but look at what we aren't doing! Two people don't have their books out! How do you not know this on the third week of school? Remember you're [insert grade here] graders. You should know this by now.

It's pretty obvious which teacher is going to get students to follow directions and feel good during class. Remember the mind is open when students feel good. Doesn't that last negative example just put a pit in your stomach?

Focusing on the negative creates a snowball effect in the classroom. As soon as you do this, the students who thrive on negativity (or normalize it due to home or friends) will multiply the negativity. They will also have a negative tone. Listen to them next time. It's pretty astounding. When you have an overly dominant positive tone, the positive students in the class will speak up, they will smile, and they will raise their hands to answer. What will happen is that the students who are used to being negative will stay quiet for a little. This tone is foreign to them. They will eventually have to adapt. They will eventually be conditioned to be positive in your presence. You may notice a vast difference between their hallway demeanor and their classroom demeanor in your classroom. They may continue the negative tone with friends and/or family (hopefully they can empower themselves to change this as well) but they will be positive in your classroom.

Listen to yourself the next time you speak. Which teacher are you? If you catch yourself being a negative Mr. Netherland, just change in that moment! We all make mistakes, teachers and students. The best teachers just know how to self-correct and move forward.

Your turn

1. When is the last time you lost your cool during a class? Describe what happened. Was this for one student, or was the whole class off task?

_____

_____

_____

_____

_____

_____

_____

_____

2. What was the impact on the rest of the class period?

_____

_____

_____

_____

_____

_____

_____

_____

Understand the Student Known to Others as the "Bad Kid"

. . . .

I am amazed how you never gave up on me.

—Timothy, known to others as a "bad kid," Grade 9,
in a letter to his teacher on the last day of school

Alan was in my third-period English class. The first time I had met him was actually when he was in seventh grade. I was covering a colleague's science class. Alan got up without permission, whipped his longer hair back out of his face, fired a wad of spit out the door, and started to walk out of the classroom without reservation. He could read the appalled look on my face as he turned his head back my direction without concern and said loudly for all to hear, "I have a 504 plan, I get breaks, look it up." He then walked out the door with swagger and without permission. I stood in shock, not sure what to do. I had been schooled by a twelve-year-old boy.

The following year, on the first day of school, Alan walked into my eighth-grade class and sat down. He didn't remember who I was but I sure remembered him. He continued to shout out without permission, put his feet up on the desk when he wanted to relax, and occasionally either fell asleep in class or had trouble staying in his seat. Other teachers expressed the same concern, even in the first week of school.

There are no bad children. Just misunderstood children.

In most classes, you will have (cough) a student who presents a challenge. Perhaps you have a higher number of students who present challenges. Either way, you have many ways to address this. I, by no means, believe any student is "bad." This is how they are thought of and described by most. I like to think of them as misunderstood children. I get excited when I spot them in class in the beginning of the year. In my head I'm thinking *Ha!* (*rub hands together*). *Let the work begin.*

You can spot them, too: the student who yells out, the student who is disrespectful to another without realizing it, et cetera. They are screaming for help. The trick is to catch them early. You know what I'm talking about: They make careless decisions, they have little self-control. There is a whole list of factors as to why one child may be more difficult to teach than the others. Let's call these students "children with challenging behaviors." Keep in mind that challenging children *want* to be known as good children. It's true. Deep down all students want to be known as the good student. For the naughty student, something just went wrong down the line somewhere, or they never had a reason to want to change.

Tips to Keep in Mind With Challenging Students

1. Children who challenge want equality. They want to be treated just like every other student. The fastest way for you to lose their respect or trust is saying their names more than others' names or in a different tone than others', or disciplining them directly and in front of the class. This will be a showdown even the most experienced teacher can lose. Speak to these children in the same tone and at the same volume that you use with the other students. Have the other conversations with them privately. They will show better behavior.

2. *Show* students with challenging behaviors you are not going to give up on them, but don't hold their hand. Encourage them to take responsibility for their behavior. The secret is to show them that you are not going anywhere and neither is your support. Challenging children almost always have instability in their family lives. Show them with your actions that you are a constant factor in their lives. Even if they mess up, hold them accountable and expect the best for next time. Ask them, "What could you do differently next time?" Build their thinking skills, and show them you are listening. Actions mean much more than words to these children.

3. Expect them to do well. Students know whether you believe in them or not. They know which teachers think and know they are intelligent. They will perform the best for these teachers. Believe in them. This is something you have to do internally. Do not think, *Oh, I hope Sarah doesn't*

> *blow it again on this test.* Instead think, *I know she will do better this time.* What you think will come out in your words, energy, and actions toward the child.
>
> 4. Find out what interests them and print out articles on that subject for them to read. The best practice that I've found works the best with students like this is finding out what interests them. When you find out what interests them and you take an interest in it, **they translate that into you caring about them and they see a way to connect with you.**

Alan used to bring a skateboard into class. Although our school had a policy to check skateboards in before entering our campus, Alan somehow bypassed this system. He wanted to hold onto it. I realized that I should use his interest to get him interested in reading. I started asking casual questions about which skaters he liked, where he skated, et cetera. I asked if he had any pictures of him doing cool skate tricks or videos I could watch. He started showing me pictures of him doing tricks after the class ended. He was really talented! I wanted to find out everything I could about his interest.

I would then print out articles about famous skaters that he would read during independent reading time. He no longer slept during this time—he was actually reading. He asked me for more skating articles and started showing me pictures of skate tricks he had mastered on the weekends or after school. This became his normal routine. I even snuck some current events in there about skate legislation, et cetera.

Shortly after that, he started taking notes in class and working with others during group work time. The other students started asking him about skateboarding and he felt like he belonged more in the classroom. With his permission, I printed out a picture of him doing a skateboard trick and hung it on our student wall. He was sheepish and at first he felt too embarrassed to have the picture displayed. I convinced him that others would like to see how talented he is. The other kids asked him to sign it. When our wall was filled up, I kept the picture hung next to my desk. He noticed and he continued to complete work in class.

His academic grade went up, he was more engaged in class, and he felt connected to our classroom. At the same time, I also placed him on an eight-week behavior (see Best Practice #14) contract that helped redirect many of his off-task behaviors, such as shouting out and leaving his seat. Yes, he still took his breaks but with permission, and he also completed classroom assignments and worked well in a group most days.

I had another challenging student when I taught in a public high school. She was a ninth-grade girl. We'll call her Colleen. Colleen loved makeup and fashion. In fact, she loved it even more than academics, because she would do her makeup and hair during every class. I started saving my copies of *Vogue* and brought them into her every week to take home and read. I didn't give them to her with any expectation of her owing me anything. I just quietly put each copy on her desk before class, and it was there waiting for her when she arrived. She knew I remembered every week. She would beam, look at me, smile, and yell, "Thanks, Ms. Pariser!" She then did her best to complete work and participate during class. Because I took an interest in what she cared about, she began taking an interest in what I cared about: the classwork. I knew she liked fashion, and respected that. Colleen took a little less work than Alan, but the same best practice was used: Find out what they're into and take an interest, by asking many questions so you'll have a way to connect, and by **listening genuinely** to what they say. Then, ask more questions. Eventually, try bringing them things that show you are genuinely interested in their interest. Their interest will be validated.

When you do this for students, they feel like you "get" them.

Remember:

- Challenging students have fragile egos.
- Challenging students are used to being known as "stupid," "difficult," or "annoying"—change this.
- Challenging students want to be trusted by adults.
- Challenging students want to feel like they "belong" in your classroom.
- Challenging students want to be known as good deep down.
- Challenging students want to be understood.
- Challenging students are used to not feeling heard.
- Challenging students want to be valued by their classmates academically as well as socially.
- Challenging students will quickly lose trust if your words do not match your actions.
- Finding out what interests a challenging student can allow a connection.
- Tiny favors or recognition go a long way with challenging students.
- Challenging students are screaming for help, but don't know how to ask for it.
- Challenging students with low academic achievement often make up for lack in academic ability by making themselves heard and seen socially. If you can help them succeed and become engaged academically, they have less of a need to be heard in other ways.
- Challenging students with high academic achievement are often just bored academically. Challenge them.

Your turn

Think back to a challenging student you have had or worked with in a classroom. Look at the list of four suggestions in "Tips to Keep in Mind With Challenging Students" on p. 62–63.

1. Which of these strategies did you try? How did it work?

_____

_____

_____

_____

_____

2. Was one of these strategies not used?

_____

_____

_____

_____

_____

3. Think of students in your classes who have problematic behavior. Do you know what interests them? What do you notice about what they wear, how they spend their time, or what they talk about that could lead to finding out about what interests them?

_____

_____

_____

_____

_____

BEST PRACTICE #13

Reward Students

I think that my actions deserve a reward.

—Dom, Grade 8

Every student loves to be rewarded. Many aren't as outspoken as Dom. If you think your students don't deserve rewards, you are probably just not giving them opportunities to succeed. Some teachers will threaten to withhold rewards from the entire class to gain power and a sense of authority. Be careful not to fall into this easy trap. If you do this, the students will think you do not want them to earn the reward, and that's not what we want. We need them to see that we believe in them and think they can achieve.

Emphasize student successes. Give them a chance. The most valuable reward is one that they have to work for. Students love to be rewarded in groups or with their friends. Make sure the reward fits how they performed, how hard they worked. Make them compete against each other to earn the reward. Your classroom will have an energy to it, and students will be focused as they are competing for the prize, or in teacher terms: doing their work and learning.

There is some controversy over extrinsic prizes for students, but I always believed that an extrinsic prize is the perfect soil in which to grow intrinsic motivation. As they work for the extrinsic prize, they will feel successful and confidence, which are perfect feelings to nurture intrinsic development.

For ideas on how to reward, do an Internet search for "behavior modification systems" to see what you find. These are the same rewards I use with behavior contracts. (See Best Practice #14: Learn the Power of Behavior Contracts.)

Tips and Ideas for Extrinsic Rewards

(These have worked for me.)

1. Technology time during lunch

2. Technology time during lunch, with a friend

3. Microwave popcorn (so easy if you have a microwave)

4. America's Funniest Home Video episode (a student requested) during lunch

5. American's Funniest Home Video episode during lunch, with a friend

6. Bookmarks

7. Teacher's assistant for a day

8. Field trip

9. Greeter privilege for a guest speaker

10. Cool pencils/school supplies

11. Popsicles (easier clean up than ice cream/frozen yogurt)

12. Popsicle party with a friend (they just sit and eat popsicles, but they love it)

13. Surprise reward—always works really well (See Best Practice #45, Surprise! Have an item or two under a box with a question mark on it.)

14. Lunch with the teacher (works well in elementary school)

Note: Any reward that can be celebrated with a friend of their choice makes it much more enticing for students.

Your turn

1. What are your thoughts on extrinsic rewards to foster intrinsic motivation?

    _____

    _____

    _____

    _____

    _____

2. Did you ever have a project in middle or high school that had a competitive edge? Did that make you work harder? Why or why not?

    _____

    _____

    _____

    _____

    _____

3. Brainstorm some additional rewards that would be fitting to your grade level or classroom.

    _____

    _____

    _____

    _____

BEST PRACTICE #14

Learn the Power of Behavior Contracts

Do you have a student with whom you repeatedly have the same conversation regarding an unwanted behavior, yet you see no change in behavior? Do you feel like a broken record with this particular student? You may need to use a behavior contract to redirect behavior. According to Intervention Central (www.interventioncentral.com), a behavior contract is "a simple positive reinforcement intervention that is widely used by teachers to change student behavior" (Wright, n.d.). I wish I had had formal training for behavior contracts in my first few years teaching.

One of the colloquial definitions of insanity is "doing the same think over and over again and expecting a different result." Unfortunately, this is what we risk when we hope that the students will change behavior as we continue to use the same talks and same consequences that aren't working.

As a general rule, the earlier you start a student on a behavior contract, the more successful the contract. I suggest starting a student on a behavior contract in the first month of school, if possible. A behavior contract's success is all about the pitch. By "pitch," I mean how you speak to the student about starting the contract.

Mistakes and Misconceptions

The most common mistake I see teachers make is complaining about the behavior but not using a behavior contract, and just hoping the behavior will go away. Although that would be so much easier, ninety-nine percent of the time, the behavior won't go away. With a behavior contract, the earlier the better, but it's really never too late to start a student on one. I once had a student on one the last eight weeks of school, and my life was so much easier after he redirected his negative and distracting behavior. I wish I had done it sooner.

A common misconception is that behavior contracts are taxing on teachers. Yes, they will take a little time, but the payoffs are worth it, times a million. Your class will most likely turn into the only—or at least the first—class in which the student redirects her behavior.

Another common misconception about behavior contracts is that they are only for students with IEPs. In reality, any student can benefit from a behavior contract. A behavior contract is separate from an IEP and made by the teacher, not the case manager. I suggest you use no more than three behavior contracts (one or two is optimal) in each class, for your own sanity. It's too much work for the teacher to have more than that. Choose your top student or two who set off the rest of the class with an unwanted behavior or two.

I've also heard teachers say their whole class is on a contract. I guess that could be, but it's highly unlikely. Behavior contracts are private contracts with select students **who need help following your normal class expectations**. The help they usually need is **motivation** to follow the class expectations. Think of the contracts as behavioral training wheels for a select few.

I've only had a behavior contract not work once, and I've used them with countless numbers of the most difficult students. I believe the student for whom it didn't work was barely getting sleep at home. Without sleep, almost nothing will work.

I heard about behavior contracts during my third year of teaching. The school psychologist was my coteacher, and she suggested we put a student (we'll call her Jamica here) on one. Jamica liked to interrupt our eighth grade class daily with a bodily noise that rhymes with "slurp." That's right; Jamica could do this at will. She actually was talented enough to interrupt the flow of a lesson almost on cue about ten minutes into our direct instruction on a daily basis. These were lessons I had spent hours perfecting the night before.

You can imagine my frustration when she brought her own bodily instrumental additions into our lesson, and always at the most focused part of the lesson. You can also imagine the wild and surprised reaction of a class of eighth graders when she did this. Her own reaction was usually the most exaggerated, as she would almost fall off her chair laughing. During our many after-class talks, she would plead innocence and say she couldn't control it. We called home, and her grandmother explained that she did this all the time in the house, she should change her diet, et cetera. Clearly we weren't getting anywhere.

How did we get the burping to stop? We used a behavior contract. It worked. This example is extreme yet true. A behavior contract is a contract you make between you and the student to redirect unwanted behaviors. Behavior contracts are your secret weapon. If a behavior contract can stop Jamica's undesired bodily behavior, it can redirect almost any unwanted behavior you'll find in the classroom. The unwanted behaviors can be, but not limited to, the following:

1. Excessive talking

2. Shouting out at inappropriate times

3. Not staying in seat

4. Making fun of others

5. Rudeness/defiance to teachers and/or other adults in class

6. Not following instructions the first time asked

These are the major ones that most teachers say interrupt a lesson. A behavior contract can and will redirect these behaviors. A behavior contract is to redirect and extinguish unwanted behaviors in order to continue with the learning.

The trick with behavior contracts is they are temporary and focus on specific, observable, and measurable behaviors, not just on "being good." Also, **they focus on only three desired behaviors unique to the particular student** you have the contract with.

It's better for the child if the behavior contract is used with every teacher that child has, but the adults all have to work together to make sure it is signed daily. Sometimes, it's only possible logistically to have a behavior contract for your class. Perhaps the success the student experiences there will bleed to other classes. The way to success with behavior contracts is giving the student opportunities to feel success by doing the desired behaviors on the contract.

How do you choose which students need a behavior contract? A student should be put on a behavior contract when your **classroom consequences are repeatedly not working** for a specific student and the unwanted behaviors are holding back the learning of the class.

A child has to truly believe you want her to succeed and you believe she can meet the goals of her contract. That's the only way a behavior contract will work. You have to be on the child's side. This may take a little change in perspective on your part before making the contract.

Behavior contracts should be cocreated with the student in order for them to have the best chances of working. The font can be chosen together, the picture can be chosen together, the desired behaviors should be chosen together, and most important, the rewards should be chosen together. This way the student takes ownership. Otherwise, you're just handing her a piece of paper.

It's helpful if you can print the contract on a colored sheet of paper, so the student can find it easily in her binder. It should look something like Jamica's contract in Figures 14.1 and 14.2. This is the contract passed down to me that was created by my mentor, Dr. Orletta Nguyen, and which I used for my most challenging students, year after year. It works better than any other contract I've tried to use. This is just a simple template she created on Microsoft Word, and is a mixture of many of the behavior contracts out there.

If the student has an IEP, one of the many great aspects of the contract shown her is that it includes percentage goals for behaviors that can be brought into IEP meetings if need be, and if the desired behaviors in the contract align with the IEP goals. For rewards, I found most boys like food and friends as the reward. Girls are a bit trickier with rewards they desire, so you may have to give them a few choices. The prizes should gradually grow larger every week. (See Best Practice #13, Reward Students, for a list of reward ideas.) If you have a student on a contract for more than four weeks, at Week 5 you return to a low-level prize, the same level as the prize for Week 1.

Figure 14.1   Front Side of Behavior Contract

Jamica's ENGLISH CLASS
Contract

Week of _____
          (date)

Week 1 GOAL Percent to reach reward: 60% = 9 boxes marked with a 3, 4, or 5

	Monday	Tuesday	Wednesday	Thursday	Friday
Be polite to all adults in room with words and actions	5				
Follow directions the first time asked	4				
Stay focused without sound disruptions during instruction time	5				

A LOST CONTRACT RESULTS IN A 1 FOR THAT ENTIRE DAY

5 = 80–100%   4 = 60–80%   3 = 40–60%   2 = 20–40%   1 = 0–20%

Source: Behavior contract created by Dr. Orletta Nguyen

Figure 14.2 Back Side of Behavior Contract

I, _____, agree to the following contract. If I am successful I will receive the weekly prize. If I am unsuccessful, I will receive a negative phone call home. I will give this contract to Ms. Pariser at the END of every class to sign.

 PRIZES!!

WEEK 1: Technology time during lunch with candy
WEEK 2: Technology time during lunch with candy AND popcorn
WEEK 3: Technology time during lunch with friend with candy, popcorn, and soda
WEEK 4: Technology time during lunch with two friends with candy and popcorn

Source: Behavior contract created by Dr. Orletta Nguyen

Each week, go over with the student what reward she is working for and the three desired behaviors. Have the student hand the contract to you at the end of each class period, and talk with her about how she did that day for each desired behavior. Then the two of you agree on a number to put in each box. For example, if Jamica follows directions the first time asked sixty to eighty percent of class time on Monday, a *4* is written in the box for that day. Most times, the student will be able to accurately self-assess what she did well and how she can improve the next day. This is empowering to a student. This takes about thirty seconds, maybe less.

Every Monday, give the student a nice new contract. In Week 1, have the student work toward getting a 3, 4, or 5 in 60 percent of the fifteen boxes. The goal for Week 2 should be about 70 percent. Week 3 should be about 80 percent, and Week 4 should be about 90 percent. You're gradually changing behavior, because that's how forming new habits works.

After this discussion, you hand the contract back to the student. She is in charge of it.

Pitching Behavior Contracts

The way you start a student on a behavior contract can make a huge difference. Are you a talented salesperson? This is the skill that will help you with a contract. Here's an approach and a script that can help.

Let's go back to Jamica. Here's what I did to start her on a contract. First, I asked her to stop by my room during lunch. You want to pitch a behavior contract when there aren't other students in the room. This is the most important aspect of a behavior contract: the sale. The reality is, you want this student to change her behaviors. You want her to *want* to follow the contract. When Jamica stopped by my room, she asked if she was in trouble. I responded, "Actually, no, it's a good meeting!" She was curious about the meeting all morning. This is what you want. If you have a paraprofessional in the class or another teacher, it's more powerful if this person can be at the meeting too, so all adults in the room are on the same page with the behavior contract. I had my coteacher at the meeting with Jamica.

You'll need a solid twenty minutes to have this launch meeting. In this meeting you will not only "sell" the student on wanting to follow the contract, but also cocreate a contract, using a template, with her. Have the template pulled up on your computer ready to personalize with the student and also— very important—**have the three desired behaviors you want already in your head or written down somewhere you can glance at.** You have control of what they are, but you want the student to think she chose them, too. So, for Jamica let's say we want these to be her desired behaviors:

1. Respect all adults in class.

2. Follow directions first time asked. (This one I love because it can cover so much.)

3. Stay focused during instructional time without any sound disruptions to stop the lesson.

These are measurable, observable, and stated in the positive. That is, they are the behaviors you *want* to see, not the behaviors you *don't want*.

Also, have weekly rewards jotted down that you think the student may like. Okay, here's what you say:

Teacher: Jamica, how are you liking our class?

Jamica: Good.

Teacher: Well, I have an idea. You know how you used to be doing really well in class and had a B+ average? That was really nice and I felt like you were enjoying class more. Didn't you like that time?

Jamica: Yes.

Guaranteed, she'll still be wondering if she's in trouble.

Teacher: I had an idea on how you can focus more in class. However, it takes a lot of work from me so if you tell others about it, they'll get jealous and everyone will want this. Do you want to hear about it? (Basically, if she tells everybody about her contract, other students will want the contract, too, and you'll be giving rewards to the entire class. Other students won't perceive it as fair—even though it is because this specific child just needs a *temporary accommodation to meet the same behavior expectations as the other students*.)

Jamica: Sure.

Teacher: It's called a behavior contract. Have you ever seen one of these before?

Jamica: Oh yeah, I've been on a contract before. I hate them.

It's fine if she says this. At this point, a student that you choose to put on a contract may have been on a contract before. If they have, you can say this:

Teacher: Oh no, yeah I know about those other contracts. This one is different. You'll love it. I chose you for this because I think you'll really appreciate it. The reason I picked you is because I noticed your behavior has been slipping and I'd really like to see your grades go up in class and I know you can do it. There are so many students that beg to be on these every year. I just can't do it for everybody. Want to hear about it?

You have to be excited about the contract. Make the student think it's an opportunity. Think like a car salesman. Your demeanor can't convey to the child that she is in trouble and that this is the last resort (which is reality). She has to feel special that *you chose her* for the contract. Students may still be a bit confused, but are often curious at this point. This is where you want them. You now have one of your most difficult students on board.

Now, pull up the contract on your computer. It's better if it's already ready to show, so you won't be scrambling around. If you have a document camera, you can project the contract as you personalize it. Students really love this. Start with letting them pick the font (any font is fine) that they like, and ask what type of things they like (dance, football, soccer, even street art is fine). Put a little picture of this on their contract. You'll use the same contract every week, so let them take their time picking a picture of their favorite singer, favorite football player, or something else. I had many contracts with a picture of Ronaldo kicking a goal. Now they are excited. At this point, explain the rewards.

Teacher: So each day, you are graded on three things. Just three! What do you think would be the best thing to change so you can focus more in class?

Jamica: Maybe my seat?

Teacher: No, I think your seat is actually fine. Hmmm—let's think. What about how you speak to our coteacher, Ms. Wish, sometimes? Do you think maybe you could be a little kinder with your words?

Jamica: Oh yeah. Maybe that would be good if we changed that.

Teacher: So do you think that could be one of the things we rate every day?

Jamica: Yes.

You do this until you get the three behaviors you originally wanted; however the students will think they actually did it and will own the behaviors more. It's fabulous. Spend time going over the rewards, and be excited when you talk about them. Then say,

Teacher: However, there might be a week that you don't make it. I hate when that happens, but because I'm putting in so much with the rewards, we do have to have consequences if you don't make your contract points that week.

Jamica: Okay.

Go over the consequences, and let them know you really want them to get the reward every week. They have to truly believe this. Have the student sign the contract; shake hands (you just made a sale). More important, you just got your sanity back—congratulations! The contract should start that day or the next. So, if you want to start a contract on a Monday, you should have the meeting on a Friday or that morning before class. It's all about the sale.

For consequences for not meeting their contract goals, use what will be most effective for that particular student. Here are some ideas:

1. You inform the student's sports or extracurricular activity coach about the misbehavior at the end of the week.

2. You call the student's parents at the end of the week and inform them. (As Figure 14.2 shows, this is the consequence chosen for Jamica.)

3. You give the student detention during lunch or after school for twenty minutes. Make sure that a detention doesn't turn into a "counseling

session" or even a "homework makeup" session. For detentions, my mentor showed me a trick of setting a timer for the time, then not allowing the student to socialize with you or anybody else for that time. If they start to do that, just walk over and stop the timer without saying anything. They will groan. Then, restart it again when they stop socializing with you or the other students in the room. Unfortunately, we need them to feel uncomfortable for a short amount of time so they will not want the consequence again, and hence will work harder to meet their behavior contract goals the next week.

One of the secrets of a successful behavior contract is **students HAVE to make their goal the first week for it to be most successful.** They need that taste of success. Really work with them to believe they can reach it. They probably will. If they do not make it the first week, they might give up on it. Then you're back to square one, because they won't want to do the contract any more, and they most likely won't follow your classroom expectations based on their behavior history.

If they don't reach their goal in the weeks after Week 1, then they receive the consequence and start over on that goal the following week. They work for that goal until they make it—and they will.

If you have pushback from other teachers who say you are "bribing" students to do well, know that's not the case. Other teachers knew I was doing something different because even children with the most severe behavior problems were displaying excellent behavior in my class. Because students felt success in my class, they felt more comfortable in my classroom and also with me as a teacher, and our relationship was healthier. This leads to increased learning. You are using extrinsic motivation to foster intrinsic motivation. Your school psychologist would agree with the theory behind this contract. This is a temporary scaffold to redirect desired behaviors to maximize learning. If you take the student off of the contract after four weeks, she may very well continue with the great behavior, because she's conditioned herself to act appropriately in your classroom. Some students need an eight-week contract, and some need even longer. When you feel it's time to take students off a contract, make it a celebration. Reward them with lunch with you and tell them how proud you are of them.

Behavior contracts can be extremely effective with children and teenagers at home to redirect unwanted behaviors and promote desired behaviors. For more tips on how to create one, see "How to Create a Behavioral Contract With Your Teen" by Rosenya Faith (2017) at www.howtoadult.com.

Tips to Keep in Mind
Regarding Behavior Contracts

- An unwanted behavior will most likely not just go away without intervention. It will most likely get worse.

- A behavior contract's success is all about the pitch and consistency.

- The earlier the better with a behavior contract.

- A behavior contract takes a bit more front work from the teacher, but the payoff is well worth it in the long run.

- Behavior contracts are not just for students on IEPs.

- Choose behavior contracts for students with whom your classroom consequences are not working, repeatedly.

- Behavior contracts are cocreated between the teacher and the student.

- Behavior contracts should focus on three specific, measurable, and observable behaviors.

- Behavior contract desired behaviors should always be framed in positive words.

- Have no more than two students in each period on a behavior contract. Otherwise, it's too much work for you.

- Behavior contracts are temporary scaffolds for the student.

- An entire class should not be on a behavior contract. Instead a class could be on a behavior modification system. A behavior contract is for your "hardest" students.

- A student on a behavior contract has to believe you really want her to succeed for it to work.

Your turn

1. Have you ever used a behavior contract with a student? Did it work or not? Why?

   _____

   _____

   _____

2. What new ideas about behavior contracts did you learn from this section?

   _____

   _____

   _____

3. Imagine that you have a student who you are going to put on a behavior contract. With a partner, describe what this meeting would look like.

   - When and where would you have the pitch meeting?

   - How much of the contract would you have finished before the meeting?

   - How much time would you allot for the meeting?

   - How would you pitch the contract so the student wants to participate in it?

   _____

   _____

   _____

   _____

   _____

Real Conversation With a High School Student

Student [to a teacher a few days before final grades are due]:   Teacher, can you round my C+ to an A?

PART 3
CURRICULUM AND INSTRUCTION

Desperate Times Call for Desperate Measures

I had this teacher in fourth or fifth grade, she was an elderly teacher that didn't have a very strong voice. She used to keep this glass paperweight on her desk. I remember it was shaped like a hockey puck, the perfect shape to hold in the hand. For some reason, her desk was made of metal. She used to pick up this hockey puck paperweight and slam it down on her metal desk over and over again to get our attention.

—Michael, age 57

How does curriculum and instruction relate to classroom management?

Curriculum and instruction is the mother ship of classroom management. If you can plan instruction that is rigorous, engaging, collaborative, and connected to the real world, your behavior problems will start to disappear. I used to spend countless hours being reactive in my classroom management. This is a slippery slope. Once I flipped how I was using my time, my behavior issues decreased dramatically. Planning quality instruction is the most effective, proactive way to have strong classroom management.

I REMEMBER WHEN....

I remember when I first started teaching at an alternative high school in South Carolina. I completed my student teaching in another alternative school in Minnesota, but it was nothing like this one. This school was for students who had been expelled from traditional high school. There were regular fights on campus (some that would happen in classrooms, which was very dangerous for teachers), drugs being both sold and used on campus, rival gang members made to be together in the same classroom, et cetera. I had multiple students who started in the middle of the year, straight from a stint in a juvenile detention center. I even had more than one student arrested for murder while I was working there. (One student was actually arrested in my classroom on Monday morning for a murder the night before.) Needless to say, teaching conditions were difficult, as most of the students absolutely did not want to be in school one iota.

Feeling unsure what the best approach was, I thought back to college when I had read Aristotle's Metaphysics. I recalled how Aristotle talked about how every single person, by nature, has a desire to know and to learn. With that as my motivation, I turned all of my efforts to instruction tactics and lesson planning. I tried to make each lesson as engaging, interactive, and hands-on as I possibly could. Good grades, a diploma, or even cool prizes were no motivation for these students. I had to appeal to their intrinsic desire to learn and be curious about the world, all while keeping their attention on learning and not on each other.

I quickly found that a well-planned lesson was the key to successful classroom behavior management. I relied on all of the principles of pedagogy I had learned in college to keep the students focused and interested for each and every one of the fifty minutes of class. Not only did the students learn, they enjoyed class and found it to be a calm and peaceful respite from their unimaginably difficult home lives and the culture of violence and poverty they were born into. I ended up being named Teacher of the Year my second year at the school and was one of very few, if any, teachers who never had any serious behavior issues in my classroom. This was all thanks to a focus on lesson planning and instruction.

—Jeff Kirschbaum
15 years' experience
The Academy of Our Lady of Peace
San Diego, California

BEST PRACTICE #15

Get Your Students Engaged: Make Learning Fun and Make It Transferable

> Thank you for helping me by changing my thinking.
>
> —Vicky, Grade 9

What is the role of a teacher? Is a teacher a distributor of knowledge or an inspirer? I always liked to be more of the latter. Students almost worship teachers who can make learning fun and interesting. Make the learning relevant to their lives. Make the content into something they want to learn, rather than something they have to learn. The best way I learned how to do this was to work with projects. When planning a project I would ask myself, *Where would they need to use this knowledge or skill in the real world?* This question forced me to make the learning real. Then, I would plan my project accordingly, so the learning was real, relevant, and exciting.

For example, I wanted my inner-city students to experience a piece of classic literature. I was becoming annoyed with the fact that they were being fed "inner-city youth" books because, people assumed, that's what they could relate to. I chose *Of Mice and Men*, by John Steinbeck, even though I was cautioned that the students might not be interested in two hillbillies during the Great Depression. *How do I get my ninth graders to want to read this book?*

To start off, I came back to the real world and put myself in my students' shoes. I thought about how the book is banned in many schools. I took that angle and printed out reasons why the book was banned, but left the title out of the write-up. I had a sheet of opinions both for and against the ban, without mentioning the book's name. After reading the write-up, the students were in. They were sold. I told them I got special permission to read the book with them (I mean, I did have to clear it with my supervisor). They were honored and chomping at the bit to know what the book was.

When are we reading? What is it?!? That was all I heard for the next day in the hallways. I gave them a few vague clues like, "One of the characters is mentally challenged and I'm certain class members will disagree on what they think of the ending!"

The students who figured out the title from the vague clues were sworn to secrecy (I knew they would tell a few since they were too excited to keep it a secret—but it was part of the fun), and they could barely keep themselves from screaming out the title. The next day I had copies of *Of Mice and Men* in the center of the room, in a wrapped box (adding another element of surprise). I had a sign on the box that read, "What could be in here?" They came in, and all eyes were on the box. Some tried to poke it. When class started, I ripped open the box, and I couldn't stop them from grabbing at the books and opening them to the first page. This enthusiasm was much different from the nonengagement and chaos of my first class, remember? We began to read. I used an audio recording of the book. I'm a strong believer in using audio for class novels (good for auditory learners, incorporates character voices, models perfect pacing, and gives you a break). I stopped the book at the exciting parts where something was just about to happen. When I pressed stop they would scream, "No! Five more minutes!" I mean, really, high school students? Yes, really.

When we finished listening to the book I asked them one question: Did George make the right decision to end his best friend's life? They were torn. They were upset. We had a class discussion, and they were told they had to choose a side by tomorrow. The class split in half. I didn't tell them what side I was on so as not to bias opinion and add an element of surprise again. While we had been reading the novel, we had also read and dissected nonfiction articles about court cases of the mentally challenged, asylums, and lobotomies. This reading and discussion provided them with background information to make their answers to my question real. Think about it: If a student felt George had made the wrong decision by ending Lennie's life, the student had to be ready to speak about the condition of asylums during that time period. This also allowed us to cover more standards (shhhhh!).

They were then asked to write a position paper or persuasive essay defending their side. There's your persuasive essay composition in those, oh yeah, dry standards. After they wrote their papers, they still weren't sure what was coming next but knew something else was on the way. Students were then placed on debate teams and told they would go head to head to see which team would win a debate about whether George Milton made the right decision. They were taught how to debate with passion, how to write note cards, how to cite, how to use textual evidence, and how to hold a formal debate. Team members were also told there would be surprise guest judges at the debate. The guest judges were students from other grades who had read the book the previous year. Of course, you could invite parents and other adults around your school to be judges, American Idol–style. These debates were usually the highlight of my year. From start to finish, it was a seven- to eight-week unit.

Enthusiasm, intense rage, rigor, and unbridled passion were unleashed from the students all for a—book. Wow. This can and will happen when you bring learning to life and make it real. You can be an inspirer.

Quick and Easy Tips to Get Students Engaged

- Add an element of surprise in your units or lessons. You want your students to be thinking and talking about your class, even when they are not inside your classroom.

- Add a competitive edge to your projects.

- Let students work in groups or pairs for projects.

- Add an element of student choice to your projects.

- Connect your units to the real world.

- Invite parents into see the final projects.

- Invite students from other grades into see or judge the final presentations of learning.

Your turn

1. Think of a project you have done with your class that went extremely well. What elements of the project contributed to that? Could you have made it even better?

_____

_____

_____

_____

_____

2. Think of a project you have done that maybe didn't go as well as expected. Why was this? Was there an element of it that was missing?

_____

_____

_____

_____

_____

3. Now think of a project you are planning in the near future. How can you make it exciting and real for your students? Competition? Guest speakers? An element of surprise? Working in groups?

_____

_____

_____

_____

_____

BEST PRACTICE #16

Research, Read, Use

Remember: Effective, engaging, and powerful teaching is being done every day all around the world. Research and find an idea better than yours or one that can help you. A majority of great teaching relies heavily on research about what methods work best. As dry as teaching research books may be, they are extremely worth reading. Instead of constantly being reactive in the classroom, you can prevent misbehavior and misunderstanding of concepts in the first place, and teaching methodology books can actually show you how. So when you have time to catch your breath, probably in about your second or third year of teaching, pick up a few teaching methodology books. Here are some of my favorites:

- *Differentiating Instruction in the Regular Classroom: How to Reach and Teach All Learners* (2012) by Diane Heacox, EdD

- *The First Years Matter: Becoming an Effective Teacher: A Mentoring Guide for Novice Teachers* (2017) by Carol Radford

- *Mentoring in Action: Guiding, Sharing, and Reflecting With Novice Teachers* (2017) by Carol Radford

- *Letters to a Young Teacher* (2007) by Jonathan Kozol

- *Positive Discipline in the Classroom: Developing Mutual Respect, Cooperation, and Responsibility in Your Classroom* (2013) by Jane Nelson

- *See Me After Class: Advice for Teachers by Teachers* (2013) by Roxanna Elden

▶ *Strategies for Implementing Writer's Workshop* (2016) by Richard Gentry

▶ *Words Their Way* (6th edition, 2016) by Donald Bear

▶ *Strategies That Work: Teaching Comprehension to Increase Understanding* (2000) by Stephanie Harvey and Anne Goudvis

▶ *The Learning Challenge: How to Guide Your Students Through the Learning Pit to Achieve Deeper Understanding* (2017) by James Nottingham

▶ *Best Practice: Bringing Standards to Life in America's Classrooms* (4th edition, 2012) by Steve Zemelman

Think of teaching as you would cooking. The best chefs are those who are not afraid to try new dishes. They can laugh at themselves when they mess up and use those blunders to get better. The more I read the research or teaching books, the more I kick myself for not having read them earlier. The time you invest in the research will save you loads of exhaustion, frustration, and energy later.

I recommend reading books on how to discipline with

▶ Best practices

▶ Positive words

▶ Proactive classroom management

▶ Practical and transferable classroom tips (seating charts, behavior systems)

The techniques described in the research work. Just think that everything you are trying to do has been done successfully somewhere else. Why not read about it?

Your turn

1. What teaching research, methodology, or pedagogy have you read or heard about in the past few years that has benefitted your teaching or knowledge of education?

_____

_____

_____

_____

_____

_____

_____

_____

2. What would you like to learn more about?

_____

_____

_____

_____

_____

_____

_____

_____

Pick Up the Pace

In addition to the common practice of using a timer to pace your lessons, you can also project a timer on a document camera for chunked portions of independent work, so students can self-monitor their own pace. A timer projected for students to see can also help with classroom management; it empowers students to stay on task for independent classwork time.

A very common educator mistake is teaching too slowly. By this, I mean spending too much time on one activity before moving on. It's simple: Pick up the pace. Today, teachers are competing with television, computers, cell phones, and music that seem to move at a zillion miles per hour. How are we supposed to compete with that if we are going only one mile per hour? Keep the students on their toes; they will give you the gift of their attention.

Here are some tricks to keep your pacing up. One of the most successful ways to keep up the pace is by planning your pace. By planning, I mean actually writing the duration in minutes of each part of your lesson on your lesson plan. Pacing is like goal setting. If you do not plan your goals in life, life plans them for you. If you do not plan your pace, the class plans it for you. Chunk, or break up, the lesson on your lesson plan. Use only twenty-minute increments at the longest for middle school, and thirty to forty for high school. Keep a timer. If the timer goes off, move on. You have most likely lost their attention or are about to. Use your best judgment, though. If the class is still engaged, keep going if you have to, but watch for glazed eyes and other signs of disinterest. They will be falling off the wagon, so to speak, shortly after.

> Keep the students on their toes; they will give you the gift of their attention.

30 minutes

The table that follows is an example of a simple, chunked, thirty-five-minute lesson plan for elementary or middle school. It is based on the work of Madeline Hunter (Wilson, 2017).

Example of *Chunking* and Planning *Pace* in a Lesson

Minutes	Lesson Objective:
	Given a collection of poems, students will analyze personification by explaining and illustrating personification in poems on graphic organizer.
5	Anticipatory Set: Watch the short two-minute clips from *Beauty and the Beast* that include many examples of personification. Ask students to jot down responses: What did you notice the objects doing in the movie that they can't do in real life? Example answers: dancing teacups, laughing water
	Share responses with neighbor, then class.
5	Model: Project a model poem with personification using a document camera. Show explanations and illustrations already completed next to specific lines in poem (to save time) about why it is personification (using metacognition) as students watch you think aloud.
	As a class, construct a class definition for personification and compare with a definition that can be found online.
10	Guided: After reading a second poem with the class at their seats, have students repeat lines after you using the SDAIE (specifically designed academic instruction in English) strategy Choral Response. Then have table groups of students work together to explain which lines of the poem contain personification and why in writing (just as you did for the model poem). Next, have individual students quickly sketch pictures illustrating personification in the second poem, as well as compose a mini paragraph about personification in it (to up the rigor, since they have been working with table groups).
10	Independent: Have individual students start to work independently to complete a graphic organizer to analyze a third poem with the same explanations and illustrations as they did for the first two poems. They can finish the paragraph for this poem for homework if needed.
5	Closure: Ask students to write down three other examples of personification on an exit slip to assess understanding of your teaching. Have students talk with a partner and share their learning with the class.

Your turn

I challenge you to use a timer next time you teach. Keep track of how long your students are in one learning modality.

1. Reflect: Was any chunk or part of the lesson more than twenty minutes (for middle school), or more than about thirty-five (for high school)? Lessons longer than these may lead to engagement issues.

    _____

    _____

    _____

    _____

    _____

    _____

    _____

2. Use a timer when you teach a few times to time each chunk of the lesson to get yourself situated to the new pace.

    _____

    _____

    _____

    _____

    _____

    _____

    _____

BEST PRACTICE #18

Use Arm's Length Voice

· ·

Here we will discuss not the student's voices, but the teacher's voice. This is a common mistake, but with such an easy fix. If you are talking to a student one on one, that student should be the only one who hears the teacher. **If you are talking to the whole class, the whole class should hear you.** As teachers we need to be smart about our voice control.

Consider being in a public library working on a paper or reading a book. Think how you feel when someone starts talking at a normal volume level to a friend. Remember that frustrating and upsetting feeling you get in your head? My thoughts usually sound like this: *Really? Do you not see me working right here?* This is how our students feel when you speak at what feels like a normal volume one on one. **Keep your voice at arm's length when speaking one on one or even to a group that is sitting around you, like in small group instruction or station learning.** This means if you hold your arm out long, your voice shouldn't be heard more than that distance away from you. It's about three feet. It is also helpful to kneel next to students to get their full attention without disrupting the overall flow.

Keep in mind: Other students out of arm's length of you shouldn't hear what you're saying, so they can stay on task.

Your turn

1. How can it benefit student learning to use an arm's length voice when speaking to one student?

    _____

    _____

    _____

    _____

    _____

2. When speaking to a small group of students, how can it benefit the class to have only that group hear your voice?

    _____

    _____

    _____

    _____

    _____

3. Have you ever been in a coffee shop or library and heard a loud talker at the next table or chair? How did that make you feel? How did that affect what you were reading or studying?

    _____

    _____

    _____

    _____

    _____

Be One or Two Steps Ahead of the Class

L et's use our imagination for a moment. You just received a call from a friend inviting you to dinner this week. You show up and your friend's house is a mess and dinner is not cooked. Your friend is frantic and looks a little annoyed. You wonder if you did something wrong. Should you help or stay out of her way? You enter sheepishly and try to make light of the situation. Now, your experience has been lessened, and your friend obviously is not ready to entertain, mentally or otherwise.

Now relate this scenario to a teacher who is not prepared. Yes, we've all been there once or twice. I remember when I was teaching a class my first year and I came to class worn out and tired. I felt like my life was a pile of papers waiting to be corrected. I laid textbooks on the desks, put an assignment on the board for students, and thought they owed it to me to do their work. After all, didn't I put in long hours for them? As Julia Roberts stated perfectly in *Pretty Woman*, "Mistake, big mistake, huge mistake." Your students will work only as hard in class as you do on the lesson. When my students came in, they saw the books and groaned, and one or two students opened them. The class soon turned into me repeating over and over again like a broken record, "Stop . . . don't . . . what! . . . no!"

If you do have to do textbook work, try this: Let the students know you spent some time finding an exercise that is important to their learning or interesting for a specific reason. Then, you can go over the lesson with the whole class and pull a group of struggling learners to a side table or another part of the room to get extra help from you as the rest of the class works independently.

This shows you did put some thought into how you are teaching. Don't insult your dinner party by cooking frozen pizza, and don't make the mistake I did by insulting your class by putting a page number, or webpage, or subject to Google on the board and praying for quiet. Teachers, that's a dangerous lesson. We've all felt like it sometimes, but if this becomes a habit the students will start to think, *This teacher is never prepared. She doesn't care about us or our learning.* As my principal used to say, "Do your homework." Be prepared.

Now imagine you are invited to the same friend's house for dinner. Everything is cooked, the table is set, and place cards are even on the table for a fun icebreaker. You can see how excited your friend is to entertain that evening. You walk in and smell dinner almost ready, and appetizers are on the table. You have your contribution in your hand (your host was one step ahead of you and let you know how to contribute), and you know this will be a wonderful evening. This is what a student feels like when a teacher is prepared mentally and phys-ically. The classroom is set *and* the teacher is obviously mentally put together.

I used to make the mistake of having the classroom completely set up, but I spent so much time and energy doing this I never took a few minutes to prepare *mentally* some mornings. This leads to disaster. Take a few minutes before your class in the mornings or afternoons to mentally prepare, calm, energize, and be ready to host your class! If you want to go the extra mile, or need to (as I did for three years), do a mental run-through of your lesson each morning or even after school the day before. I would have my lesson plan in front of me, lock the door, turn off my cell phone, and practice my lesson. This would point out holes like, *Oh, I will need markers on the desk for that. Wait, I need notes on the chart for that.* The rehearsal made me much more confident when I was actually teaching the lesson, ensured that all the materials were ready, and made me always prepared. I felt the students knew I cared and was prepared. This takes only a few minutes. I recommend it in your first few years of teaching until it becomes natural and effortless to you. Think of yourself as a performer doing a dress rehearsal.

Tips for Demonstrating to Students That You are Mentally Prepared

- If students are in groups or with partners, have a basket or bin on the tables with materials they will need for the day. You can even have the worksheets they will need that day so you can avoid downtime as you pass them out. A rookie mistake is spending too much time passing out papers. I have noticed the time passing out materials (including papers) is one of the

(Continued)

(Continued)

most frequent times the students have the opportunity to lose engagement. Students will be disengaged and start having side conversations. Don't let this happen!

- Have notes for your presentation written beforehand, depending on how you do your delivery. A prepared PowerPoint or digital presentation also works. Then, you can just write side notes, visuals, et cetera as you are speaking to keep momentum.

- Know how long each part of the lesson is, and keep a timer. Show students you are both on a schedule. Students will take as long as you give them more often than not. The times should be reasonable and public (project a timer for the class if your technology allows, announce the time remaining often, write time remaining on the board).

- Tell the students what they will be learning that day and why in the very beginning of the lesson. Make it relevant. Be brief, clear, and motivating.

- Have the materials you will need to deliver the lesson in your teaching area, wherever that may be, so you will not have to say, "Wait, where did I put that . . .?" Think of your teaching materials as props for your lessons.

Your turn

Make a T-chart of two different lessons you have taught. On the left, describe a lesson where you were unprepared. On the right, describe a lesson where you were prepared. Next to each, describe how you felt while teaching each lesson.

1. Now jot down how the students reacted to each lesson.

   _____

   _____

   _____

   _____

   _____

2. Only you know what works best for you. How can you make sure your lessons are prepared every morning for students to learn?

   _____

   _____

   _____

   _____

   _____

Keep Everything Contextualized and Do Projects!

> We work as a group. It feels nice to have freedom.
>
> —Zac, Grade 8

My first few years teaching I felt like I was drowning. I was barely keeping my head above water. I was planning lessons late the night before and would come to work exhausted, short fused, and dragging my feet. I couldn't think about what the students were going to do even a week in advance because I was too busy making phone calls home, grading papers, and dealing with the mental exhaustion and frustration that comes with disciplining and yelling all day. I remember putting textbooks on the desk, assigning a page, and wondering why the students weren't engaged. *Kids just don't want to learn,* I would think daily. Or I would make a few worksheets and hope that kept them busy the whole period. I was more a police officer than a teacher, patrolling the room for noise and misbehavior. They wouldn't listen to me anyway, so I thought maybe if they saw the lesson for the day in print it would help. I just wanted them quiet and learning.

Looking back, what would have helped me immensely is taking the time to plan projects from start to finish. I could have then launched the project and let the students become more empowered learners while I took more of a facilitator role. We live and we learn.

Project-based learning is powerful. Period. Have you ever felt like I did my first few years? You were probably going through the motions without passion, excitement, or purpose. Was it after a breakup, after you suffered a loss, or during a transitionary phase of your life when the larger picture was unclear or blurry? One of the most important things we must remember is that students are human beings, too. They get angry, they get scared, and they get unmotivated, for most of the same reasons we do in life. Most important, they need a larger picture or purpose for what they are doing. They don't want to just complete the worksheet.

I know you can relate. Think of how excited you have been, or how motivated you were when you were planning a fun trip or vacation. You probably were excited, got many tasks done at once and quickly, and put thought and care into the planning. Everything you were doing was for a specific purpose. You knew the outcome. You knew the bigger picture. Your motivation was contextualized.

Students think the same way. Think of their "trip" or vacation as the final project. Do they know what they are working toward? Will they be building something, showing off something to parents or the community, debating against classmates, presenting something to classmates or other classes even? What's the overall goal of the unit? Once they have their goal established, they will understand how the learning is contextualized and will be more motivated to work more diligently. Your job will quickly slide into the role of the facilitator: guiding the students to their goal of the finished project.

If you put in a little extra work in the beginning of a unit of study to develop the big picture, not only will you increase learning and the quality of the lessons, but also the engagement will be much higher. An added bonus is that behavior issues will severely decrease, and students will become (dare I say it) inspired. If you plan lessons without a bigger picture, expect your students to drag their feet and act as you would without a larger picture, goal, or purpose in your life.

This means before you launch a unit, take some time to develop the bigger picture. An idea is to wait a week or so until they feel confident with the start of the work before you tell them what the entire project is. This can prevent students from backing out completely because they think it's too much. Or, describe to your students what the bigger picture is right away. Inform them of what they will they be doing, creating, performing, or competing for in this unit. It's really your judgment call as to when you reveal everything, but it should be done within the first week. Don't just give them the end project, but also let them know why they are learning the content. This does take a little extra time in the beginning of a unit, but it will dramatically help with engagement and student satisfaction throughout the entire rest of the unit. It will ultimately lead to your greater satisfaction as an educator. Engaged students lead to a satisfied teacher.

Problem-based learning works the same way. The difference is that the students are asked to *solve a problem* as their overall goal and present their elegant solution, and the learning is contextualized. This is different from the overall goal of *creating something* in project-based learning. Depending on your task, you can decide whether your unit is more geared toward project- or problem-based learning.

With project- or problem-based learning:

▶ Behavior issues significantly decrease.

▶ Students become more empowered and inspired to learn.

▶ Your role becomes more that of a facilitator than a leader.

▶ You must do more planning up front.

▶ Learning becomes contextualized in the bigger picture.

▶ Students are asked to create something or solve a problem.

▶ It usually takes two to eight weeks to complete a unit.

Here is an example of an introduction to a unit of study where students know the larger picture.

Teacher: Students, today we are going to be starting our class novel. Why are we reading this particular book? This novel will help us understand and most likely disagree with one another about what it means to be a true friend, empathize with someone with a mental disability, and understand life during the Great Depression and see aspects of it you probably won't learn in a history class. The more we read, the more likely it is that we will develop a love of reading that will help us in high school and beyond. As we read the novel, we will get to do so many things! First, we will have class discussions throughout. Then, we will get to decide how we feel about the ending of the novel. After we read the book, we are going to be doing an exciting class project, so be sure to pay attention to the different characters and all of the details of the book.

So let's see what the students just heard. They just heard they are going to be held accountable as the class reads the novel. They also heard that you are looking out for their best interest. You also kept part of the project a surprise so they actually cannot argue and say the project is boring or stupid. They also know you have something larger planned. You have them hooked. Think of this introduction as someone telling you that you just won a trip to a surprise tropical location and to start planning. If you add the element of surprise to the mix, the suspense not only keeps your students motivated but prevents them from arguing against the project. The trick is to be as excited as you want them to be. They are going to be looking at your clues to see how cool the project is. You are the salesperson for this project.

Your turn

1. Can you remember a time when you weren't sure why you were doing an assignment or didn't see the larger picture? How did that make you feel?

_____

_____

_____

2. Did you ever do a project or unit as a student that you still remember really enjoying? What made it enjoyable? How can you transfer this to your own teaching?

_____

_____

_____

3. Do you agree that contextualized learning maximizes performance? Why or why not?

_____

_____

_____

4. How can you make learning contextualized, engaging, and stimulating?

_____

_____

_____

Challenge and Support Students

· ·

I loved your class the most. It was the most challenging of my classes to keep up in. You gave me the extra support I needed and I knew someone believed in me.

—Karen, Grade 9

Our teacher is always looking out for us, ya know? That's why he's the best.

—Jimmy, Grade 11

Consider Goldilocks from *Goldilocks and the Three Bears*. She couldn't sleep in the bed that was too hard, or the bed that was too soft. She had to find one that was just right. Some students are like Goldilocks. They may not respect a teacher who is too easy, nor do they like one who is too difficult. The goal is to be "just right." To be just right, first challenge your students; then support them where needed and encourage them as they feel success. Let them know the lesson today will be challenging; then show them how you will help them.

Let's look at a specific example. Say you are teaching poetry. An easy teacher may have students conduct their own research on poetry. Perhaps this teacher would make it more fun by letting them share with each other, or giving them some other enjoyable but low-rigor assignment. Fun, but what is the purpose? In contrast, a teacher who is too difficult may say, "Write a two-page narrative poem. This will be graded. You have the computer to help you." (Note: If this is where your students are, then that is a different story.)

A just-right teacher would have a challenging lesson presented in clear parts manageable to students. First, she would show students models of narrative poems. Then, she might break down parts and elements of a narrative poem quickly. (The key is also to not give too much help, or you will belittle the students' abilities or give them an excuse to be lazy.) The class could then brainstorm possible topics of narrative poems. Finally, the teacher could explain how the assignment would be graded (referring back to the great examples in the beginning) and give time for the students to work on the project. Finally, she could also pull up a group of struggling learners for additional help as the other students write and have access to computers for help. See the difference?

This teacher will earn respect because the students are challenged and given help that they may need, but not too much. The students are also instructed on the grading process, and they will feel like they *need* the teacher's help because the assignment is difficult and they would like a high score.

Ultimately, you'd like to see your class rely less and less on you as the school year goes on. The hope, by the end of the year, is to have your students perform, learn, and converse as a community of learners *without* you. It's then you know you've inspired a change greater than yourself. You will succeed and will no doubt be respected if you do this. However, before that time comes, challenge them. Make them need you just enough, and be sure to support them. They will grow with your nourishment.

Remember to keep taking scaffolds away from them throughout the year. For example, in the beginning of the year with groupwork, you may choose to assign each group member a role that defines how each will contribute to the group. This is a scaffold to effective collaboration. By the end of the year, your students shouldn't need these roles assigned and will hopefully be able to work in a group effectively. Expect them to work more independently and to create better products as the year progresses. This means you give them less academic support and set the expectation that they perform at a consistently higher level. If they falter, be there to give them the support they need. Keep doing this, and they will grow.

Remember:

▶ If your class is too easy, your students will cruise though and you will have less of a connection with them, because they won't need you for support. Students may feel like they are missing out on learning what they should.

▶ If your class is too difficult without support, students will become frustrated and distant and feel like they aren't heard.

▶ The goal is to have challenging curriculum with supports such as collaboration, engaging projects, small group instruction, checks for understanding, and use of best practices to engage and challenge students throughout the learning journey. Challenged and supported students feel respected.

Your turn

1. What are the qualities of an instructor who is too difficult? How can this make a student feel? What about an instructor who is too easy?

_____

_____

_____

_____

_____

2. What are some specific teaching strategies, practices, and habits a just-right teacher would use? How would this make a student feel?

_____

_____

_____

_____

_____

3. What type of instructor do you see yourself as now? How do you want to see yourself in the future? Are there gray areas?

_____

_____

_____

_____

_____

BEST PRACTICE #22

Take Risks in Your Lessons

Great teaching is all about risk taking. My greatest memories as a teacher are of when I took the biggest risks. By taking a risk, I mean planning something more than what you have seen the students do or could even imagine them doing. When you take risks, you have to visualize what success will look like. Then, you teach and inspire your students to rise to your vision. When you take risks there are only two things that can happen: Your students will fly or they will fall. Here's the secret: They almost always fly. You have to teach them the skills they need, inspire them, believe in them, and then let go. They will fly. The biggest risk taking usually took place at the end of the year for my class. That's when they were ready.

The first time my students really flew, I'm not sure if I slept the whole month before. I kept wondering what would happen if they didn't perform. It was the last project of the year with my eighth-grade class, and they were in groups. Each group was assigned a concept that we had learned during the year. They had to create a poem to perform with props, movement, and gestures in a spoken-word manner. I thought about who to invite as an audience, and I decided on inviting a younger grade. My students panicked. They didn't think they were ready. I let them practice a bit more, and they started to build up their confidence. They were looking great! My mentor suggested I go big, really big. She asked why I wasn't just inviting the whole school. I hadn't even thought of that. So I did.

I sent out an evite to make it a formal event. Each administrative member received a private invitation. Classes responded one after another, and so did the administration. As a class, we checked the evite every day on the document camera. They knew the pressure was on, big time. To say the class was engaged was an understatement. They knew this was bigger than I was or even we were now. The day of the performance, the entire auditorium filled with parents, administration, students, and teachers. My students looked like deer in headlights as they watched class after class come down. They couldn't believe everyone came to see them. They rocked the stage! Although they were a bit terrified at first, it showed them they were worthy of attention. They received a standing ovation and were beaming ear to ear afterwards. They were the talk of the school! I could sleep again. They flew.

Another time I took a risk was when a student in my class broke a class computer. I had at least three options: one, to pretend it didn't happen and move on; two, to have a very harsh talk with everyone about computer care, make threats, et cetera; or three, to make this situation into a life lesson and take advantage of a teachable moment. I chose the hardest but most powerful option: three. My rationale was that only one student misbehaved. I knew who I thought it was. I knew he wouldn't confess, and I knew that I could not really prove he did it. I wanted the class to understand the severity of the situation, I wanted them to understand learning is number one, and I wanted to determine how we could come together to move on from there. I wanted to build a community.

I pulled them in a tight circle of chairs and explained what happened. I explained that we could have the computers taken away from us, every period. They all started pointing fingers. I stopped them. I said I didn't have an answer and I needed their help. (This was half true.) I knew that in all honesty I could have privately sorted this out with our technology department, since this sometimes happens. However, my gut instinct was to turn this into a *learning experience*.

We brainstormed for a few minutes in a circle as a class about how to raise the money to fix the computer. We came up with the idea of a car wash. We made signs during lunch, and I pulled a few strings and got permission for my classes to all hold a car wash at our school on a Saturday. I was a little fearful that nobody would show up, so I assigned shifts. The morning of the car wash, I came early. I didn't see any students. I took a deep breath and had faith that they would come. One by one students arrived with a smile. Before you know it, we had many of my students, and even one of their dogs came. I saw a caring side of this tough class that I had never seen before. The students actually raised over $300 that morning and felt more connected, and that class became a cohesive family. The message became clear: We will help each other out during this school year. They had each other's backs. I took a risk, believed in the students, and hoped for the best.

Your turn

1. What message do you send your students when you take risks with them?

_____

_____

_____

_____

_____

2. What is the worst that can happen if you take a risk and student response flops?

_____

_____

_____

_____

_____

3. What message do you send your students if you do not take risks with them?

_____

_____

_____

_____

_____

BEST PRACTICE #23

Know How to Prepare for When You Just Can't Be There

As a teacher, you often see your students more than you will see some of your own friends. Chances are your students see you more often than even most of their friends. Let's face it; they will grow comfortable seeing you every day. More than anything, children learn to trust reliable adults. One of the most effective ways to earn trust is to be reliable and consistent. However, we also know that life happens—so how do we miss a day of school without losing our students' trust?

First, don't miss too many days. Students' worlds revolve around themselves. They are not adults yet. So, they may not grasp the full concept that life does happen, people get married, kids have appointments, and some days you may just not be there.

Planned Absences

If you have a planned absence, an effective method to reinforce the trust with your students is to have a talk with them the last five minutes the day before you are going to be away, even if it is only for a day. Let them know you are very sorry (one or two students may joke and applaud) but most will really, wholeheartedly appreciate that you valued them enough to let them know. Share with them why you will not be there (if it is student appropriate). Sharing should be limited, purposeful, and honest. Let them know you will be back the next day, if that's the case.

Example: Students, I want to speak with you seriously for five minutes, and I need your attention. My best friend is getting married this Saturday, and the wedding is in Virginia. I have been invited in the wedding and have to take a flight tomorrow morning. Unfortunately, I will not be here tomorrow, but will be back on Monday. Now, let's talk about how we respect a guest teacher. What type of behaviors do I expect when a guest is in the room? (You may get some students asking questions here about the actual wedding, and that's all right. Personalize it. Show them you are a human, not some teacher just "ditching out" on them. They will end up appreciating you more for this.)

Some of my former students remember four years ago when I flew to Virginia to be in a friend's wedding. They remember this because I told them about how she and I became friends and why it was important that I went. I told them a funny story about an incident that happened at the wedding when I returned. They enjoyed being a part of my life for a second. If I had not had this conversation, I would have been just another teacher who missed another day. A conversation such as this will not only empower the students with knowledge but also show the students you value their learning and their trust.

Unplanned Absences

It happens. Be careful not to let it happen too often. Students remember when you are not there. I have a hard copy of a letter waiting on my desk (a hard copy is always the way to go for a substitute if possible) or e-mailed to the sub that states that I am sick (I usually specify what type of sickness if it is appropriate) and what type of behavior I know they will show. I ask the substitute to read it aloud to the class, as well as project it on the document camera for the students who benefit from a visual representation.

The main idea is to treat the students with respect and as if they are part of your family. Teacher absence can be a shock for students. Make your face a familiar one they will see every day.

Your turn

1. What are you really telling the students when you let them know in advance that you will not be there?

    _____

    _____

    _____

    _____

    _____

2. How do you think this makes the students feel?

    _____

    _____

    _____

    _____

3. How could this actually prevent discipline issues with the substitute?

    _____

    _____

    _____

    _____

Use Creative Discipline

Something miraculous happens when you start to get comfortable and confident: The students pick up on the vibe that you have their best interests and learning at the forefront of your mind. This means if you take a few minutes to handle a discipline issue with the class, they listen and take it seriously. Every once in a while something a student does conflicts with the values of the entire class and learning environment. (Because I do full-class discipline so rarely, the students know it's a pretty big deal.)

However, most discipline can and should be handled privately and quickly between you and the student.

In one of my later years teaching, I remember three times when I put my foot down to help facilitate a better learning environment:

The first time was when the students were saying "no" to me in the middle of the year after I asked them to do something that was beneficial to their education. I asked them to work with certain assigned groups in certain areas of the room and had major defiance in the classroom. I had preassigned groups based on skill set so students could help each other learn content. The students wanted to work with whom they wanted to work, and where they wanted in the room. Now, students usually listen very well to my instructions, but if one student starts to challenge, it can spread like wildfire. This happened rarely, but when it did, I made it very clear to that student privately that this was not going to continue (and called the parents to discuss what happened.)[1] I knew if I let

---

1. High school teachers have conflicting views on whether and when to involve parents. I usually do if the student needs the extra support, especially in the ninth or tenth grade. High school students can get very defensive when parents are in the middle. The biggest win is when you can empower the students to change on their own. Use your gut to decide whether or not to call parents.

the challenge go, I would have one heck of a year with students deciding when they would follow directions.

I want my students to know they cannot be defiant, but that we have a positive relationship where they can express their feelings in a respectful and articulate manner without being judged or scolded. It is always necessary that they be heard. You don't always have to act on it if they misspeak. You are teaching them the respectful way to speak, not waiting for them to make a mistake. My guide was always this: If disrespect or malice was intentional, that's an issue. If it was unintentional, they are learning, and I teach them how to correct their words or actions. They know there is also a time, place, and way to phrase their concerns, and that I will listen. Defiance and open communication are two different things.

In this instance, the students were being defiant and holding up learning. Two strikes! I extinguished that fire quickly: I made it very clear to the students that saying "no" was not a choice they had at the time, what I was doing was best for their learning, and I would listen to any concerns after class. For now, the learning was going to continue regardless, and choosing to work with their friends was not an option they had today, although they would have it in the future. I said all this with a very stern and serious face and did not lose control of my emotions.

At the end of class, I left five minutes to recap with the class why I had been disappointed that day. I let them tell me, not the other way around, so they could take ownership of it. (Sometimes I even do a turn and talk and then they tell me. This is also a powerful check for understanding.) They recapped that I was upset because they were outwardly defiant—which stops learning in a classroom. I made it very clear how much I value their education, and it's not fair to others to not have a solid day's learning because their classmates choose to be defiant to a teacher. It's important that the class understands specifically why you become frustrated or stern, or they may repeat the same mistake again. Before the recap, a few of the students thought I was disappointed because they wanted to work with their friends, which was not the case. The reason you are frustrated should always be about what's in the best interest of the student and the learning.

The second time was when a few students were rude to me one week. This is absolutely not going to fly in my classroom. I exaggerated my reaction and did raise my voice that day. I made it clear I was not angry that they were overly talkative, but I was angry at the tone and demeanor they were using toward me. I used an "I" message:

> I want to be very clear why I am frustrated with not only a few students but the class as a whole. I value respect. I always try my hardest to give you the most respect I can. You are making a conscious choice to be

rude. I need you to understand this is not the correct choice and turn it around. Am I angry that you were too talkative today? Not really. Although it is not acceptable, it happens sometimes. That's just how a class works. However, you do not have to be rude. I need you to understand the mistake you made and stop it, now.

Then I was deliberately very quiet during the rest of the class period (I had to fake that part since I have an extremely forgiving heart by nature), and let them know how much I valued respectful and polite words and actions towards the teacher. After that, they understood. My students became extremely polite and exceeded my wildest expectations after that.

The third time was when we had an issue with stealing. Personally, I've always felt that this is one of the worst things that can happen in a classroom. If you catch it when it's small, you can prevent it from becoming a larger issue. In my first year teaching, my laptop and cell phone were stolen from my classroom. A student rummaged through my personal bag and took them. (I felt as if he had stolen my teaching credential, because I no longer felt like a teacher.) I felt violated, hurt, and betrayed. I cried. I was confused. Who did it? How could one of my very own students do this? What if I never find out who did it and I have to look at every student's face as a suspect all year? With administration's help and some investigation, I did eventually find out who did it, and he received consequences based on district protocol. However, I know now never to let stealing escalate to that level.

In my seventh year of teaching, a parent brought me chocolates on Valentine's Day. I thought it was so thoughtful, so I showed the class with a cheesy smile plastered to my face and set the candies upfront. I was beaming! After class, the sweets were nowhere to be found. *Really, are you kidding me?* I knew I was not going to find them. I considered some of my options before reacting in front of the class. (*Deciding* how to react is a superpower that comes with years of teaching.)

a. Tell the whole class what happened the next day, knowing they would all point fingers at each other, and either blame an innocent child or not ever figure it out, so the students know they can take from me. I turn into the teacher who gets things taken from her.

b. Do a private investigation and get the chocolates back.

c. Do something a bit more creative.

I opted for c. I realized I would not get the chocolates back, but I also had to show the students I was the teacher. When push comes to shove, the bottom

Deciding how to react is a superpower that comes with years of teaching.

line is that our job is to protect the safety, morale, and learning of our students. I decided to blow up the situation to prove a point. I was the teacher. I taped off the exact spot where the chocolates had been with an outline, similar to a body sketching the police would do at the scene of a crime. I borrowed some yellow police tape from our custodian, and taped around the front of the room where the chocolates once sat. I had a few miniature bright orange cones I placed around the area. I took all the chairs from under the desks and put them in front of the "crime scene." I also wrote "Why the chocolates?" in large letters on our flip chart easel, but I kept a blank sheet of paper over it, so the students couldn't see this question when they entered the room. (This was an idea from a college tutor in my room who helped with creative ideas. Note: College tutors often have the best ideas.)

I had a very serious look on my face as the students entered, sat silently in the chairs, and stared at the strange scene in front of them. I posted a prelude exercise on the document camera that asked them how they felt when some-body they trusted took something from them. I had already left a sticky note on each chair, and they all responded in writing on the sticky notes about how hurt and betrayed they would feel. I then (still seriously) explained that I felt the same way. I let them know that up until now, I trusted the class. I also said that it is really important to me that they feel like their materials and belong-ings are safe as well (remember, it's not you versus the class). Then, when they understood my concern, I flipped the chart paper on the easel and the students saw the question, "WHY THE CHOCOLATES?!?" They had trouble keeping their giggling under control at this point, as I still kept a straight face.

I explained with a serious tone that I had called the FBI to do a thorough investigation of the crime scene, and I would need other information. I said the thief could confess anonymously, and my goal was to restore trust and safety in the class. I thought I knew who did it before we started the "investigation." However, during the lesson, as the rest of the class was giggling about making such a big deal about chocolates, a different boy than the one I suspected had his arms crossed, could not stop shaking his foot, and was red in the face. I could feel his discomfort. *Interesting,* I thought. I had all the information I needed. I spoke to the boy privately after that. He would not confess, but I knew. I took down the crime scene afterward, and the boy was never a discipline issue after that, as he had been prior to this incident. He knew it was my classroom. I also heard him say to his friend once, "I'm an honest man now." I knew I wasn't going to get the chocolates back, but I decided to use the theft to help me win over the class.

Would I have done this if something of value were taken? No. The reason nothing of value has been taken from my classroom since my second year is because I stop the little crimes: the missing markers, et cetera. Little crimes usu-ally add up to bigger crimes.

Today, nothing is locked up in my classroom. This is a decision I make to let the students know I completely trust them. They notice. You are welcome to make your own decision regarding this. I still completely trust my students. They know I am in charge. Would another teacher have handled it differently? I would assume most likely yes. However, I went with my gut. I felt very safe afterwards, knew who took it, and have not had even a marker disappear since.

Trust your instincts on how to monitor behavior creatively, or run it by another teacher first. Just remember that teaching is like a dance; everyone has his or her own style, rhythm, and flow, and we all value different aspects of the craft. Try something, and if doesn't work, it's okay. Take risks and let yourself mess up. That's the only way to learn. It's just a mistake, and you will try something else next time. Don't be afraid to be creative. Your students will appreciate it more than traditional behavior management. I solved the chocolate mystery in just fifteen minutes without ever having to raise my voice. What would you have done?

Your turn

1. What can you absolutely not tolerate in the classroom? Things that are not tolerated should not be specific behaviors but a value system that is being jeopardized. How do you let your students know this with your actions and words?

    _____

    _____

    _____

    _____

    _____

2. Have you told your students how the things you don't tolerate negatively affect learning? How can you explain this in a tactful way that puts their learning first?

    _____

    _____

    _____

    _____

    _____

3. Think of the last time you had to discipline a full class. Would this have been an opportune time for creative discipline or not? Why?

    _____

    _____

    _____

    _____

    _____

BEST PRACTICE #25

Vary Levels of Noise in the Classroom

Noise level is extremely tricky to get right when you first start teaching. I remember my biggest failure as a student teacher was attempting to get control of the noise level of a classroom. I had a class of twenty-five eighth graders. I asked them to stop talking and be silent to start the lesson. They didn't. I raised my voice thinking that would help. It didn't. I thought, *Maybe they just don't know what silence sounds like.*

I decided to go to the extreme and show them that they could be silent. I walked up and down the aisles and gave them each a piece of scotch tape. I said half-jokingly (I was also making the mistake of trying to be their friend as well), "Use this tape and I want you to hear what silence sounds like!" The kids were having a field day. They taped up their mouths, waving their hands in the air and forcing humming sounds out of their noses. I now had twenty-five quieter, taped-faced students. Just then, my supervisor walked in with a guest. Now, there are many times that a teacher worries if she is doing the right thing. As soon as I saw my supervisor's face, it was not a question: I had messed up. She summoned me to a meeting later that day and asked if I was doing an experiment. I knew very well that putting tape on my students' mouths was not in my lesson plan. I said yes, knowing that I had to figure out how to control noise without any office supplies. I'm thankful I was not dismissed from my student teaching semester that day.

Alternative Tips and Ideas
for Controlling Noise Level

- **Get a box fan.** This is a quirky trick, but it works. In my eighth year teaching, I always had a fan somewhere that I could turn on. The louder the better. It kept students working for hours on end. There is something soothing about the sound that keeps students working, silent, and calm. It is especially helpful during any silent activity, such as a test.

I turn it on discreetly as soon as they start reading silently or take a test. I point it toward the wall so they do not feel the breeze (this is key), and something subconscious kicks in and they start working, silently. If you tell them you're doing it to keep them silent, it may not work. Point the fan away from them, flip it on fast, and walk away. They usually don't even notice but start working silently as if I had pushed *their* on button. I put it on the highest setting. The white noise of the box fan also drowns out the chair squeaks, heel clicks, and other odd distracting noises that can break the silence.

- **If the room should be silent, then *you* shouldn't talk either.** Instead of verbally responding every time a student whispers, talks, or breaks the silence, just put your finger to your mouth to signal the noise level that you want. Every time you talk, unfortunately, *you* are breaking the silence, which is elevating the classroom noise level. A look and a few silent signals can do wonders to maintain the calm, silent classroom that some students need to perform.

To keep your class silent (during testing for example), you could say, "As a class, we know that some learners need a silent environment to do their very best. Let's respect each other and keep the entire class silent the entire time. I really appreciate how you respect each other's learning needs. I am sure your follow classmates will appreciate the silent time as well. If you need anything, please raise your hand and I will help you."

This shows the class why they should remain silent, that you are putting the needs of the entire class first. On the other hand, you know some students will need help, and you are willing to help those students. Any student requiring help in any way can simply raise a hand, and you can answer them quietly and discretely. Remember your arms' length voice here. During testing, turn that voice into an even quieter voice. You are meeting *all* students' needs in the classroom.

- **If you are playing a game, let the students get loud,** not out of control, just fun loud. Let the students' energy and enthusiasm fill the room. That's what makes a game fun! Give the students guidelines, or set some limits such as these:

   ○ No arguing with each other or the referee (teacher).

   ○ Do cheer on your team.

   ○ Remember that this game will help your learning.

You can write the guidelines on the board before you begin so you can have a written reminder to point to if they accidentally break a limit, which they very well may do accidentally if they are that excited. (Just remember that you, the teacher, are always in control.) Have you ever been to a really quiet football game? Exactly. Games, especially competitive ones, are more fun with a little noise.

- **If the students are working on an assignment, let them ask each other questions.** I explain the expected noise level to my class like this, "As you work on this assignment, the only talking I should hear is a whisper to your neighbor if you have a question. I want to make sure you have the help you may need. Other than that, please remain focused on the assignment." A few students may need a few reminders; give them a reminding look or motion with your hand that they should be writing.

Be careful not to overreact to a little bit of noise. When we overreact, it tells the students that we are not in control. We are not presenting calm and controlled leadership. We should always give off the image that we are in control.

Your turn

1. Think back to your favorite class. Did your teacher allow you to talk or even get a little loud? Did you feel like that teacher had control of the classroom?

_____

_____

_____

_____

_____

2. How do your students know which noise level is acceptable during certain activities?

_____

_____

_____

_____

_____

3. What is your personal opinion of noise level? How can voices help a classroom?

_____

_____

_____

_____

_____

BEST PRACTICE #26

Make Groupwork Work

....

We all learn from each other.

—Mary, Grade 8

Groupwork can be your biggest ally or your worst nightmare. If you ask students, they will almost always respond that they love working in groups. This may be because

- ▶ They like the social aspect of working with other students.

- ▶ They receive the help they need without having to ask you.

- ▶ It's easier to do an assignment with help from other students.

From a teacher's point of view, groupwork is beneficial because

- ▶ Students can learn social skills while working together academically.

- ▶ Students will ask you fewer questions because they have each other to ask for help.

However, groupwork can go sour very quickly. I find that every class is different. Some classes work very well together and some do not. Groupwork calls for more than just pushing desks together.

Tips for Making Groupwork Work

- **Consider how you want to group the students.** There are many ways to group students. Think about the goal you want them to accomplish. Is the assignment harder than what they could do on their own? If so, do hetero- geneous grouping. This means that you will have students of different skill levels together. This way, each group has a mini teacher to help them. If you do not group this way, all the low-level students will sink together. This is a nightmare for everybody. You could also let the students work in pairs, or in groups of three. Groups of four to six are usually the most productive, and the larger size gives them more power to perform.

- **Arrange group seats before students enter the classroom.** Arrange desks and chairs for groupwork before the students walk into the room. A lot of the success of groupwork is a function of how well the desks are arranged. If one desk is pushed out to the side, that student may subcon- sciously feel as if she is not part of the group. Perhaps even give a group the option of sitting on a carpeted floor in a well-liked or comfy corner of the room. I usually don't force students to sit on the floor. That just seems cruel. (Some girls feel uncomfortable sitting on the floor in skirts, it hurts some larger students' legs, et cetera.) If you give them *the option*, one or two groups will usually jump at the opportunity, even in high school.

- **Give each student a role.** Make sure all students are carrying their own weight. For example, one student could be the motivator. Another student could be the recorder. The third student could be the acknowledger to make sure everyone is participating. You can also assign a group leader who reports to you. I've also had groups and didn't assign roles to let the natural strengths surface organically. It's really all about what your tasks are, what age you're working with, and knowing your students.

- **Provide both written and verbal instructions.** Groups will usually fall apart only when they do not know what to do or are not held accountable. Make sure there are written as well as spoken directions to the groups. Desks are usually arranged all around the room with groupwork, so it's a good idea to have a set of written directions or procedures for each group of students.

- **Use a rubric and a daily point system.** If needed, you can give students a participation grade or points each day. Before they start the groupwork, go over a written rubric showing how they will be graded during groupwork. A rubric with examples will prevent arguments. Be sure to actually go over and teach the rubric before the assignment. If you quickly score them in class (if a participation grade is based on work produced and behavior), and they see the points immediately and in writing, this is very effective in either maintaining the stellar behavior and work completion for the next day, or empowering them to change their behavior the next day in groups.

Sometimes you can have your students pick partners or groups to work with. But this can leave some students feeling left out. If you are going to have students choose groups, there's a strategy you can use to make sure everybody feels included. When there's a student whom the others naturally don't choose for their groups, it's usually because of the student's inability to work well in a team. The student rarely can identify this and rewords it as, "I like to work alone." It's okay for a student to work alone for some tasks, but in the world today we need students to also know how to work in teams and get a job done. These are 21st century skills.

When I have one of these students in my class, I usually ask her the day before which student she works well with in the classroom. You'll be surprised whose name she'll give. It's usually different from what you think. I'll do this in casual conversation.

So, let's say Amy is the student-who-is-never-picked for groups. Amy tells me in conversation that she works well with Darin. Then, I'll put a sticky note on Darin's desk asking, "Will you ask Amy to be in your group when I have the class choose groups today?" I'll hold the note there for a few seconds, wait until the student says "yes," and then **I'll crumple it up and throw it away so Amy never sees the note**.

When I announce it's time to choose groups, Darin walks over to Amy and asks her to be in his group. Amy will most likely be sheepish and shy. She'll say sure, maybe shrug her shoulders like she doesn't care. Don't look over at this point. Amy will look to see if you had anything to do with it. Do your "teacher things" for a few minutes, and let the students get settled into a group together. Now, Amy is in a group, feels good that she belongs, and will work better. You also most likely will not have any behavior issues from Amy while she is in the group, since she now feels like she belongs. Darin feels good about himself too, and it's a win-win.

If you don't have time to have the conversation the day before, you can skip a step, choose a good role model in the class, and ask the role model to choose the student. I suggest using the sticky note because kids hear everything, and this method is most powerful when the students don't know we actually set it up; that way everybody feels like they belong. I've even used this strategy in high school effectively.

Your turn

1. What roles could you give each member of a group for a project?

_____

_____

_____

2. What is the benefit of choosing groups? What is the benefit of assigning groups? When is one more beneficial than the other?

_____

_____

_____

3. What data other than classroom grades could you use to assign heterogeneous groups for a project? How can this help every group succeed academically?

_____

_____

_____

4. Is there a student in your class who is never picked for groups? How does this student react during groupwork in your class? Would you want to try the strategy above? Why or why not?

_____

_____

_____

BEST PRACTICE #27

Let Their Creative Juices Flow

Creativity engages students. Creativity also frustrates traditional teachers, because we most likely did not use creativity for learning while we were growing up. It forces teachers to think outside of the box. The key to engaging students is allowing creativity to flow while supporting students in their learning.

Have you ever seen Ken Robinson's (2007) TED Talk, "Do Schools Kill Creativity?" It's a powerful talk that explains the importance of creativity in the classroom. I highly recommend you watch it together with a few colleagues, if you haven't seen it already.

It is best to encourage student creativity in well-planned lessons. When you bring creativity into your lessons, you will often engage the reluctant students, since they are not restricted in their learning.

Tips for Infusing Creativity Into Lessons

- For projects, give students choices (some more creative than others) on how to present their final project.

- Use multiple engagement styles in your lessons to allow creativity in students (see Best Practice #28).

(Continued)

(Continued)

- When students show creativity, praise them, so other students see you value this in your classroom.

- If students have an idea to add to your unit or lesson, speak with them during class or ask them to stay after class to discuss the idea and listen. Students most often have the most creative ideas. Explain to them why or why not their idea will work, so you encourage creative thinking in the future.

- Use your resources: Use online resources, ask a friend, or even use social media to ask for creative input on a lesson or unit. I find Twitter has a large group of dedicated professionals in the teaching world. I've tweeted for advice many times and have given advice to many educators in turn.

Your turn

1. What are your thoughts on the value and importance of creativity in a lesson?

    _____

    _____

    _____

    _____

    _____

2. In your opinion, does creativity decrease or increase academic rigor? Why?
    Try to give specific examples.

    _____

    _____

    _____

    _____

    _____

3. What is the most creative project/unit/lesson you've ever come across? How
    did the students respond to it? How much did the students learn?

    _____

    _____

    _____

    _____

    _____

BEST PRACTICE #28

Teach to Every Different Type of Learner

I enjoy this class because it's very interactive.

—Sarah, Grade 9 (an intrapersonal
learner, ironically)

Wouldn't it be simpler if everyone could learn from just a worksheet, a lecture, or a computer? Unfortunately, the world isn't like this, and neither is the classroom. Not everyone is the same type of learner. Students learn in many different ways. An experienced teacher knows this and will add tasks for different engagement styles to a lesson to accommodate all learners in the classroom.

I remember my first job interview. It was for a prestigious high school in a suburb of Philadelphia. They told me to create a thirty-minute lesson on anything I wanted in the language arts content. They told me that my audience was eleventh-graders. My real audience during the interview was six administration members. I thought long and hard about what I wanted to teach, but didn't spend as much time thinking how I was going to teach it. This was a rookie mistake.

I decided to do a lesson on Shakespeare's works. I entered the room with a transparency bulleting his plays. I lectured for twenty minutes on his life from note cards. I was shaking. I went through his life, answered a few questions from my fake student audience composed of adults, and had them complete a worksheet on what I had taught them so well. I wasn't hired. Big surprise.

Upon reflection, I realized that, like many new teachers, I was showing the class how smart I was. I was distributing my knowledge. Let's fast-forward seven years and see how I would do it all over again.

I would probably start by asking the class what they already knew about Shakespeare and jotting down what they said on the board or screen to show them that what they say aloud is important. Then, I would show an engaging, short (two- to three-minute) video clip introducing Shakespeare, and ask them to write additions for the list on sticky notes as they were watching. I would then ask the class what they learned from the short clip. (You could also ask them to write what they had learned on a K-W-L chart.) We would share what we had learned and get a class bank of collective prior knowledge to continually refer back to. Then, I would pass out a timeline with a few of Shakespeare's works and life events filled in, and a few they would have to find in resources and articles I would provide for them on credible online resources or on a mix of printed-out documents such as biographies, informative articles, and even poems. This way students could also practice code switching to read different genres of texts. They could work in groups or with partners.

Later, they could write a summary of what they learned, and I could do a short recap of Shakespeare's life and work, using the knowledge they found in their group research to summarize and to make sure we were all on the same page. At the lesson closure, I would ask students to share with a partner what they learned about Shakespeare from the lesson. Finally, we would share as a whole class and add to the class bank. Together, we could cross out information from the prior knowledge that we had learned was not true. They would have a visual representation of what they had learned in just one period.

Do you see the difference in this lesson? This is just one of dozens of ways to teach this concept and cater to different engagement styles. All different types of learners would be engaged and learning. In contrast, the first lesson would not suit learning except for linguistic or auditory learners. You would lose more than half the class, or they would pretend to pay attention but not comprehend as much as they could another way.

Hopefully, your teacher prep in college has covered Gardner's theory of multiple intelligences ("Multiple Intelligences," 2016). There's a bit of discussion now about whether these are actually intelligences or engagement styles (e.g., Fletcher, 2015). Let's call them engagement styles. It works. Once I started including more than one type of engagement style in my lessons at the same time, more and more students were engaged at the same time, in the same content, but for different reasons.

Multiple intelligences theory is not just for elementary or middle school teachers. High school students include the same range of types of learners.

They will most likely be these types of learners their whole lives. According to Howard Gardner, there are eight types of ways people learn:

1. **Bodily-Kinesthetic** learners are engaged in learning best when some movement is incorporated into the learning. Bodily-kinesthetic students learn the best by *doing*.

Ways to incorporate this type of learning into a lesson:

▶ Total physical response (students move their body to the learning)

▶ Activities where students move around the room

▶ Pantomime

▶ Charades

▶ Scavenger hunts

▶ Exercise

2. **Visual-Spatial** learners are people who learn best when they see the content.

Ways to incorporate this type of learning into a lesson:

▶ Short clips of videos (I never go longer than five minutes)

▶ Pictures

▶ Drawing assignments that let students visualize the learning

▶ Realia

▶ Graphic organizers

▶ Making maps

▶ Posters and displays

▶ Creating a mental image

3. **Musical** learners are people who learn best when content is in sounds, tones, or rhythms. Musical learners are also quick to spot patterns in tones and rhythms.

Ways to incorporate this type of learning into a lesson:

▶ Playing a song that goes with the lesson

▶ Having students compose a song or jingle with the content

▶ Creating a cheer with the content

▶ Tapping out a rhythm or cadence to the learning

▶ Playing sounds that go with the lesson (your iPhone has sound apps, or you can download off the computer)

4. **Logical-Mathematical** learners are people who learn best with logical and scientific thinking and deductive reasoning.

Ways to incorporate this type of learning into a lesson:

▶ Solve a problem using numbers or mathematics

▶ Create a timeline

▶ Create analogies

▶ Solve brain teasers

▶ Conduct scientific experiments

▶ Construct a graph

▶ Compare and contrast

5. **Naturalistic** learners are similar to kinesthetic learners. They love the outdoors and learn best when they can feel, touch, and hold items. Naturalistic learners have an innate appreciation for the world around them.

Ways to incorporate this type of learning into a lesson:

▶ Go on a nature hike

▶ Bring realia in from nature (such as rocks, plants or flowers) to incorporate into a lesson

▶ Give these students an outdoor area to read/complete work

▶ Identify and classify objects from nature

▶ Listen to audio recording of nature sounds (you could play this in the background as they are working or reading)

6. **Linguistic** learners are people who learn best with words, written or spoken.

Ways to incorporate this type of learning into a lesson:

▶ Socratic seminars

▶ Classroom debates

▶ Lectures

▶ Group conversations

▶ Written responses

7. **Interpersonal** learners are people who learn best with and from others. These students also read others' emotions very well and communicate and respond appropriately. Interpersonal learners enjoy the social aspect of learning.

Ways to incorporate this type of learning into a lesson:

▶ Work with a partner

▶ Conduct a student survey

▶ Tutor a classmate

▶ Participate in a group discussion

▶ Students teach students

▶ Groupwork

8. **Intrapersonal** learners are people who learn best by themselves and know themselves as learners very well. Intrapersonal learners are often independent.

Ways to incorporate this type of learning into a lesson:

▶ Independent work

▶ Worksheets

▶ Personal goal setting

▶ Diary or journal entries about the learning

▶ Self-evaluations

If I go into a lecture, I space out after fifteen minutes. I need to see stuff. I'm a visual learner. Before I learned about this theory, I used to just think I wasn't smart, because I couldn't retain as much by listening as others could. But it's not true that I'm not smart, and don't let your students think this. Your students need you to respect their preferred way of learning.

A great way to do this is to give your students a survey or quiz in the beginning of the year that identifies multiple intelligences. Google "multiple intelligence quiz," and you'll find one. Explain to your class that this testing is solely to help you teach them effectively. This will help ease tension and also encourage parental support, since parents will know you are looking for their student's best learning style. Also, you will have this information to use with your lesson plans. Students can also be more than one type of learner. For example, a student could be equally dominant in both visual and musical learning.

How do you use these in a real lesson? My greatest lesson plans always include activities that allow for at least three engagement styles. Actually go through your lesson and list where you use each engagement style if you need to. It will pay off in the long run. If you can include more styles, wonderful. The more, the better. If you go through a lesson and you find its activities incorporate only one or two engagement styles, beware! Including as many engagement styles as possible will help more students in your classroom and ultimately lead to fewer behavior problems and more focused learners.

Below is an example of a very simple lesson plan with at least three different engagement styles:

Example of Lesson Plan With Different Engagement Styles

Lesson Objective:

Given notes and a sorting activity, students will apply knowledge of fiction versus nonfiction.

MINUTES	ACTIVITY	ENGAGEMENT STYLE
5	Anticipatory Set: Respond: Why do people read books? Respond, turn and talk, share with class. (Ask about textbooks if responses don't include "to learn facts.")	Interpersonal
5	Model: Show two piles of books, one of fiction and one of nonfiction. Include the class textbook in the fiction pile. Do a think-aloud of characteristics of each pile. Ask students to share characteristics of each pile. Make a chart showing student responses; you will fill in the gaps in next segment of lesson.	Visual
10	Input (teacher explains; students take notes): There are two general forms of writing.	Linguistic

FICTION	NONFICTION
"fake"	"real"
meant to entertain	meant to give or relay information and facts
has a sequence of events/plot	nothing made up
made up or created by author	"how to" books
can be based on an actual event	science books
may have pictures to paint a picture	history books
	biographies
	usually have pictures to show information

(Continued)

(Continued)

MINUTES	ACTIVITY	ENGAGEMENT STYLE
5	Quick Sorting Activity With Group: Sort big piles of books into fiction and nonfiction, and put a sticky note on top with purpose of each type.	Kinesthetic
15	Independent Reading: Ask students to think, while they are reading, about whether their independent reading book is fiction or nonfiction and why. Have them write an answer to this question on an index card: Is your independent reading book fiction or nonfiction and why? Collect the cards, turn and talk, share.	Intrapersonal
5	Closure: Turn and talk: What are the two main types of books and why do people read each type? Share.	Interpersonal

Your turn

1. Print out or reflect back to a lesson you have taught that went either poorly or so-so.

   _____

   _____

   _____

2. Label where you appealed to each type of engagement style. The more the better, but you don't necessarily have to hit them all.

   _____

   _____

   _____

3. Do the same for a lesson that went very well.

   _____

   _____

   _____

4. Analyze the difference. What could you add to each one to appeal to more types of learners?

   _____

   _____

   _____

BEST PRACTICE #29

Have NO Doubts, But Be Prepared to Have (Just a Few) Lessons Flop

I magine you just signed up for your first ever whitewater rafting trip. You've never done this before but heard it may be fun. Inside, you are pretty terrified. *What if we hit a rock? What if I fall in? What if I get hurt?* Your mind races into worst-case scenarios. *I mean people have been hurt before, right? What if I'm one of those people?* You may even start to back out, or think of backing out. Then your guide, Tom, shows up. Tom begins to talk about the dangers of rafting. He mentions that he's new at the job but he knows how to call for help if needed. He's not kidding. He reads what to do from some note cards he has prepared. You can tell he's a bit unsure himself but tries to assure you with, "Don't worry we're all in this together." How would you feel in this situation?

This is exactly how students feel when teachers seem to have doubts that their students will succeed in a specific task. Instead, be the experienced whitewater instructor: They smile, they are at ease, and they know the boat will be okay (or they say so). They model courage for the team. Carry the belief that your students will succeed, even when they do not have or show this feeling themselves. They are looking for you to do this. Be their whitewater instructor.

The great news is that unlike lessons in whitewater rafting, when our classroom lessons flop, we aren't risking our students' lives. I've learned just as much from flopped lessons as from lessons that went well. Both can be valuable tools for you. The trick is that when a lesson flops, take a breath, get some water, carve out some time, and reflect. I've flopped lessons, and every teacher you know has flopped lessons. Some just talk about it more than others. The best teachers use the flopped lessons as a learning tool rather than a setback. If you have a coteacher, it's most powerful if you debrief together. In your reflection or debrief, ask yourself or each other:

- Was the lesson well enough planned? Always start with the lesson plan. Don't start with the students. The student behavior is usually a result of the lesson. Was the plan too easy or too hard, was there not enough talk time or too much teacher talk, or was more collaboration needed?

- If the plan was solid, the time was chunked, and the rigor was just right, then what else went wrong?

- How can you use this flopped lesson as a learning tool?

Real Conversation With Eighth-Grade Student

I discretely tried to take out my Invisalign while my head was turned to eat some candy.

Student: Are those your dentures?

Me: No, I'm 34.

Student: So they're not?

PART 4
OTHER ADULTS AS RESOURCES

There Are Better Ways to Have Administration Support You Than This

My ninth-grade French teacher got lost finding the classroom, as it was his first day at the school on the first day of the year. He walked into the room late and asked if this was the ninth-grade French class. I was quite the class clown back then, and quickly told him that the room he was looking for was at the complete opposite end of the complex—about ten minutes away. He ran out of the room like he was on fire! About thirty minutes later he came back into the room, led by the principal, whom he had to ask for directions after I directed him toward the gymnasium.

—Stephan, age 43

What do other adults in the school have to do with your classroom management?

Much of your satisfaction with your teaching career will be based on the adults with whom you work. The happier you are, the happier your students will be. Most teachers who absolutely love their school do so because they love the adults they work with. They've invested time to create respectful and supportive relationships with their coworkers.

Hindsight is 20/20. *I'll be real with you: This was probably my biggest mistake.* I always invested so much time in my classroom and students that I let the adult relationships suffer. I invested a lot of time in my coteaching partnerships, because that was part of my classroom. If I could help you learn from my mistake: Invest time in all adult relationships around your school environment.

I REMEMBER WHEN....

I remember when in my second year teaching critical skills at the middle school level, a parent came into my classroom, and—with little knowledge of my program or students' skill sets—looked me in the eye, and told me that her daughter didn't belong in my class and that she would be giving me a year to try to see any growth in her child, but that she remained doubtful of my class being of any use to her daughter. This deeply saddened me, because she saw only my students' disabilities and completely disregarded their strengths. With my optimistic outlook, I decided I was going to demonstrate my effectiveness and my students' capabilities, including those of their daughter. Critical skills classes are comprised of students with moderate to severe disabilities. In my class we had students ranging from those with outward disabilities, such as cerebral palsy or Down syndrome, to students with more invisible disabilities, such as intellectual deficiencies. I worked hard with my students, helped them meet and exceed their IEP goals, and did my best to create an honest and welcoming dialogue with this parent.

During my seemingly noble crusade to connect with this parent, I gave her my cell phone number so she knew I was always available to discuss her daughter's progress or troubleshoot problems. I started receiving calls well after 9:00 p.m., when I would receive angry voicemails and texts from this parent. The mom would also send me aggressive e-mails, leading me to feel like I was missing something or doing something wrong.

During meetings, the family would attack my colleagues and me. They would talk about my students' physical differences and make assumptions about their capabilities. These statements were both mean and unfounded, as I and our many advocates and specialists saw that their student was indeed making progress and working at a level comparable to that of her peers. I would leave these meetings feeling depleted and disrespected. Finally, I asked for support from my administrative team and learned to set clearer boundaries. I now answer texts and phone calls and respond to e-mails only during office hours.

It is my hope that the strategies I learned from this experience can aid new teachers when their own students' or families' actions make them question their abilities.

Tools to help keep your sanity intact when working with difficult families

1. **Set clear boundaries from the beginning.**

   My experience taught me that when I made myself too available, some parents would overstep obvious boundaries (in this case calling and texting late into the night). I allowed that to intimidate me and felt like I needed to answer right away, which then opened up the dialogue for even more harassment.

   Send out a welcome letter and lay out expectations and boundaries at the beginning of the school year. Some of the guidelines for communication can include what hours you are available by e-mail or phone. You can refer to the guidelines later if needed, and parents won't feel like you're creating the rule just for them. You have other students that need your attention just as much as the difficult cases, and you do not want to expend all your energy on one family. It is depleting and does not set healthy guidelines for teacher–family interactions.

2. **Create open communication.**

Make sure that you are transparent with your families and are in communication with them about their child's progress. I also have created communication binders for families who would like more detailed accounts of the day. This also provides two-way communication where families can respond and update you on various matters, such as dentist appointments or that their child didn't get enough sleep the night before. I always let parents know from the beginning that they are essential to their child's success and thank them for their partnership.

3. **Track data and stay organized.**

If it isn't recorded, it didn't happen. Keep a running record of student work in a folder with student work and learning objectives.

Also keep a log of all interactions with difficult parents. When I had a parent who was on the border of being abusive toward me through angry e-mails, constant calls, and texts, I started a file that helped me document the interactions, and it helped me feel confident that if it the parent ever went too far, I would have evidence of my experience. It is also important to be prepared to back findings of student progress with student examples and assessments. I have found that color-coded folders make it easy to find what I want to provide to the parent and what I need for my own records. These little organizational techniques help me keep my standing in high-stress meetings.

4. **Do not take things personally.**

I am the first to admit that this one of the most challenging things to do, but it is imperative. Usually when a family is upset, they are worried about their child, especially if they haven't yet accepted that their child has special abilities or needs. You are merely the person they see related to their concerns and disappointment, and the easiest person to blame. All too often, they are overwhelmed by the situation, and unfortunately you may get the brunt of their reaction. This does not make you any less of a great teacher! All teachers, no matter how amazing, may end up getting a high-stress parent or student advocate at some point in their career. Hopefully, these tools can be your safety net to stay afloat.

5. **Listen without interrupting, and pause before responding.**

Everyone likes to feel heard. It is important to hear your families and validate their concerns, even if you do not agree with them. A family's perception is their truth, and it is essential to honor that. Showing empathy and letting the family know you are trying to connect with their words and experience is key. This also helps you not be reactionary and feel like you need to respond right away when asked a question in a high-stress meeting. You can take your time, sit in the silence, and practice key phrases that will be mantras such as, "You make a good point, let me think about that," or "I respectfully disagree."

No need to over explain yourself; this can add to the heated interaction. My school psychologist really helped bring this concept home for me when he said to let parents climb their own mountain of angry. Often, they will climb back down on their own, and your listening may help speed this process along.

6. **When reporting behaviors, take emotions out of your report.**

    Use and show concrete examples, and avoid making statements that could be subjective (e.g., "the student was acting aggressively"). Instead be specific and state only the observable facts (e.g., "the student pushed another student with his right hand"). When reporting negative behaviors to a parent, try to also point out something positive (e.g., "the student improved recovery time after a meltdown," or "the student was able to comply with a direction"). You want the student and family to know that you are on their side while still addressing the behavioral needs.

7. **Focus on the positive.**

    For every challenging, high-stress family, you will have several that support you and realize what a good teacher you are. It can be incredibly challenging, but try to celebrate the good and the fact that there are other families that love and appreciate you. The same year that I had this challenging case, I had another parent rally all my other families to nominate me for the Excellence in Special Education Awards. I kept their entries close to my heart to remind me of my effectiveness when times got tough. When handling an upset family, it is easy to get lost in trying to please them and lose all the positives in the process. Keep a positive evidence drawer in your desk, fill it with student cards and family letters of recognition, and pull them out whenever you need a little boost. I know this has been a great asset to me on hard meeting days.

8. **Be gentle with yourself; everyone makes mistakes.**

There are times that you will drop the ball or make a mistake. It is important to recognize that as long as you are doing your best and working to do right by your students, that is all you can do. If you are a perfectionist like me, it is hard to not beat yourself up for the one *i* you forgot to dot or *t* you forgot to cross, but I learned that even the best teachers sometimes make missteps. This is how you learn. If you do find that you made an error, it is best to just own up to it, apologize for the oversight, and move forward being your awesome teaching self.

9. **Find advocates and support within your teaching community.**

Teachers need advocates and support, too! Never meet with a parent or advocate alone where you can be cornered or put in an uncomfortable position. Having someone you trust at the meeting can make you feel empowered and help you keep from being undermined. I had a case almost go to Due Process—every teacher's biggest fear—and we had a meeting to discuss the facts of the case. I invited my school psychologist because he had a friendly smile and a comforting demeanor, and I looked at him whenever I felt the heat from the tension of the room. It is important to identify your support system on campus.

Equally helpful is finding guidance and direction in areas that you have yet to experience. Facing the unknown, I asked a seasoned colleague who had been through Due Process what to expect. She gave me a rundown of her experience and highly suggested that I have my data organized and easily accessible. This helped me know what to bring with me to the meeting and made me feel more prepared.

10. **Practice self care.**

A challenging case can make you feel like you are giving more than you have. You cannot pour from an empty cup; therefore it is paramount that you take the time you need to recuperate. Do not forget that you are a person with passions outside of teaching, and it is important to nurture those other parts of yourself as well. Identify your happy place, and carve time out of your week to visit it. You need to feel whole in order to be effective in the classroom or when working with a difficult family.

I hope these tips assist you on your path toward being the wonderful teacher you are meant to be! Know there will be days when you feel like an imposter. This is normal; most teachers have these days. The important part is to refer to these strategies and take care of yourself until you feel like the confident inspiring educator you truly are.

—Jennifer Zimmermaker
Education Specialist
Mesa Verde Middle School
Poway, California
9 years' experience
Nominated for Excellence in
Special Education Awards
Poway Unified School District

Learn How to Win Over Parents

For some of us, the word *parents* has always been that seven-letter p-word. As new teachers, we often fear the phrase: *student's parents*. Why is this so scary? When we first start teaching, they are probably older than we are, and chances are that the only information they have about us is filtered to them through their child's perspective. Just hope that child respects you.

A valuable lesson I learned through years of teaching is that parents need to be and can be your best friends. They can be a valuable resource. When a parent respects and admires you, most likely the child will do the same. And sadly, if a parent feels the opposite, more often than not the child will also do the same. How do you get the parents on your side? My mantra when communicating with parents ("dealing" with parents has such a negative connotation) is this: *They are just doing what they think is best for their child.* Most parents act out of love and concern. If you repeat this mantra you can understand where they are coming from and empathize with them.

Tips for Communicating With Parents

1. **Communicate early.** Introduce yourself in the beginning of the year at open house, mail a postcard home, make a phone call, have a parent mixer, et cetera. The goal is to introduce yourself first, before the parents

hear about you from the student. Chances are you will most likely need the parent's help later down the road.

2. **Like their child.** Parents or guardians will never side with you if they feel you do not really care about their child. Most likely, they raised this child. They saw the first steps, heard the first words, taught the child how to ride a bike. They love the child. You are only seeing a limited view. If they feel you do not like their child, you will not win. Show concern for each student's situation and progress in your class. Be able to speak of at least two strengths of each child you teach.

3. **Be able to defend their child's grade.** Parents and guardians want to understand. If they are upset with a grade, they will ask for documentation. They will most likely not care about the numerous hours you spent on your one hundred other students. Most often, they only care about their child. Care about their child enough, too, to have documentation of grading in order, and work samples. This is your job.

4. **Offer support to their child.** Be ready to let the parent know that you are there to help the child succeed. Do you offer tutoring? Podcasts of lessons? Office hours? E-mail support? (Be sure your district/school allows this.) How are you extending your help to the students?

In any grade level, you want to stay in touch with parents. If you have a positive rapport with the parents, if and when you have a behavior or motivation issue, your job will be a lot easier. Ninety-nine percent of parents want to be in the loop. If they do not, it's usually because they are used to hearing negative messages from the school, they don't know how to fix the problem, and they feel like a failure. Why don't you change that by calling home for something great that their student does? Believe me, those parents will be on your side when you need them in a few weeks. Parents will most likely support you if they like you. If they only hear from you when you have bad news, they will most likely not like or support you. Think of a bill collector. You only hear from them when there is bad news. Nobody likes bill collectors.

Here are some creative ways to stay in touch with parents throughout the year. The key is to have high-volume, low-density communication. You want to contact parents often with little bits of information. Then, they can never say that the teacher does not make an effort to contact them.

Tips for Creative Ways to Stay in Touch With Parents

- Send a postcard home during the summer introducing yourself and saying how excited you are to be their child's teacher. Make the first step.

- Make parent invitations to send home with each student when you have projects to show or presentations. Parents love being audience members.

- Invite parents to come for read-alouds. Students can increase their reading level and comprehension by reading to parents.

- Invite parents to come in to help with bulletin boards. Have them write inspirational messages to their child on the board.

- Have a parent-only e-mail list that sends out reminders for tests and for classroom and school events. Then, you only have to write one e-mail to communicate with lots of parents at once.

- Have parents make copies.

- Get or make a stamp that requests a parent signature, and stamp it on top of important assignments or test and quizzes. Add an extra point to their scores for students who bring back the assignment with a parent signature. Parents love to know what assignments their child is completing.

- Have parent guest speakers if they can speak about your unit of study.

- Invite parents to come in on a peer-editing day. Parents will love to give input to students about their writing.

- Invite parents to chaperone field trips.

- Have a classroom career fair with parents of students. Each parent can have a table and talk about what he or she does every day.

- Invite a parent to come in to lead a station if you are adventuring to station learning or small group instruction.

- Invite a parent to work with a small group of struggling students or one struggling student.

- Invite a parent to read to the class. The students will appreciate the new voice in the room.

You can't go wrong. A parent will never be angry to be included in the learning experience. You may want to explain to the class the day before why the parent is coming in so that students behave with their guest. I would say something like this:

Tomorrow, class, I have invited Mrs. Smith, a parent, in to _____. I would not invite a parent into every class, but I trust this class is mature enough to have a guest. It is important that you say "good morning" to Mrs. Smith, and understand that she is dedicating her own free time to help our learning. Make sure you also thank Mrs. Smith for the time she is giving our classroom.

Your turn

1. What is an event or learning activity you have coming up where you can invite in parents? How can they help the learning in your classroom? Does a parent work for a company that can donate supplies to a project?

_____

_____

_____

_____

2. What are some low-effort ways you can communicate with parents via apps (such as Remind) to keep them in the loop of what is happening in your classroom?

_____

_____

_____

_____

3. Who are your star parents who can advocate for your classroom? How can they help you with field trips, open house nights, projects, et cetera?

_____

_____

_____

_____

Know How to Make Coteaching Work

. . . .

This section is dedicated to my mentor mentioned in the dedication, who showed me the beauty of coteaching when it works.

In education today, you most likely will have to work with another adult in your room. This could be a one-on-one aide who is paired with a particular student. Some schools have college students serving as tutors. Or, you could have the opportunity to experience the mother of all adult teaching partnerships (drum roll please): coteaching. This is when two or more teachers (usually only two) work together to teach a class or classes of students.

If you have a resource or support specialist in your classroom, as the general education teacher you are the master of content, and the other adult is the master of modifications, scaffolds, accommodations, and interventions. This means that the other adult should know best about what individual students need based on the learning goals on their individualized education programs (IEPs). With classroom management, however, ultimately you want to take time in the beginning of the year so the two of you are on the same page with your behavior plan for the classroom, so you do not always outrank your coteacher when decisions must be made, and the two of you can truly be equal in this realm.

Ninety-nine percent of teachers have a difficult time with coteachers at some point in their career; it's natural. Think of your college dorm mates. Unless you were very lucky, you probably have some not-so-delightful stories to tell of those persons, since you were living so closely with them. It's similar to coteaching. Not only are you with your coteacher every day, you are also working toward a common goal: making sure your students learn to their fullest potential. I have had coteachers on both ends of the spectrum. The difference was not so much who they were (although that is a large part of it—how well you two "sync and flow"), but how we learned to interact with one another. My mentor once told me to think of it as a marriage. Can there be a successful, happy marriage without rules and boundaries?

Many teachers in coteaching pairs that I spoke to in many different schools thought it was hopeless. They resorted to just ignoring the conflict, since it was a work partnership and not a personal one. However, this may be the worst way to handle coteaching. It will make coming to work every day miserable. And it will blow up eventually. The students are also much smarter than we all think and will notice tension in the air. Who can learn in that environment?

On the other hand, successful coteaching partnerships are powerful, delightful, fun, and exhilarating. You get to share the joy of the students every day with someone. There is someone there when Juan makes that hilarious comment (teaching stories just aren't the same after it happens), there is someone there to bounce ideas off, and much more.

Tips for Successful Coteaching

1. **Recognize and use your coteacher's strengths.** Every person has different strengths. It is far too easy to focus on a person's weaknesses. Believe me, he is doing enough of that work on his own. Does your coteacher have a great reading voice and can make different characters sound interesting? The two of you could plan for him to read aloud to the students. Is your coteacher very meticulous? Instead of thinking this trait is annoying, see if he would like to be in charge of a detailed job in the classroom, such as taking roll or grading multiple choice quizzes. I always found both parties in the room were happiest when they were using their strengths to help the class as a whole.

2. **Let your coteacher know when she did a great job with something, no matter how small or large.** Everybody wants to be praised. Research shows that employees who are ignored are the most likely to be dissatisfied with their jobs (even more than employees who are criticized). The most satisfied employees are those who are praised. Let your coteacher know when she did a great job delivering a lesson, dealing with a student, or coming up with an idea. Chances are that she will continue these behaviors, and your classroom will be a much more pleasant place when "mommy and daddy aren't fighting."

3. **Keep your coteacher in the loop.** You and she should plan together. Both of you will then be on the same page. I was one of the pioneers of coteaching in my school and advised many coteaching partnerships to help them succeed. When a partnership was not happy, these were the most common complaints:

   a. She doesn't carry her weight.

   b. She doesn't tell me what she is doing until the last minute. (This makes the other partner feel unvalued, unprepared, and purposeless.)

   c. He cannot control the class, so I have to do everything. (Most likely these coteachers are not using each other's strengths to work together.)

   d. I feel undermined by my coteacher.

4. **Recognize that coteaching is a relationship.** My mentor once gave me some very wise advice: *Serena, you're entering an arranged marriage.* The truth is that you have to treat this partnership as carefully as you would a romantic relationship if you want it to be successful. All of the elements of a successful relationship can be applied to a coteaching partnership. Why? This is because it is a very close relationship, under constant stress and tension, and the partners are working toward a common goal.

   Just think: What would work in a relationship? That is probably the answer to what would work in coteaching. For example, if you felt like your coteacher did not carry his weight, you are probably not communicating your classroom needs (just like personal needs in a relationship). As silly as this analogy may be, it works. Keep this mantra going on in your head: What would work in a relationship?

5. **Realize that you cannot change who your coteacher is, but you can ask him to change specific behaviors that may affect the learning of the class.** Everything should be focused on that: Does it negatively affect the learning or morale of the classroom? If you feel it does, bring it up respectfully (never in front of students or during class).

6. **Don't fall for the "mommy" "daddy" trap.** When dealing with student discipline, and you will, make sure the teacher who disciplined a child is the one to address the behavior or have the conversation with the student afterward. If one teacher disciplines, and another has the conversation, it sends mixed messages to the child that one teacher is mean and one is nice. This dichotomy will cause the child to favor one teacher over the other, or play mommy/daddy with the teachers. The coteachers will not appear as a united front.

(Continued)

(Continued)

For example, if a student acts out and is disciplined by one teacher, the student may seek a more sympathetic ear from the other teacher. The second teacher can say, "I'm sorry you feel that way. I want to make sure you address these concerns with [name of teacher who disciplined]." Do not engage the student in a conversation, because he needs to see the same teacher as both the disciplinarian and the understanding teacher. He needs to see well-rounded teachers who are united.

7. **Do your share of the paperwork, grading, copies, and phone calls.** You should make his job easier. Or, if you are the lead teacher, be clear on how you want him to help. An overworked teacher is an unhappy teacher. Coteachers who split the workload are a solid team. Perhaps the second adult in the room makes all of the phone calls home? Or, you could give him a class set of notebooks to grade? (Just make sure the grading is consistent among all the classes the two of you teach.) The lead teacher should figure out how to split the work; then it usually works better if the second adult always does the same task, so there is not confusion on how it is done. For example, the second adult could always call parents, or the second adult could always grade the reading notebooks. Even better, the second adult can always grade a certain class's quizzes or tests and give the teacher a list of grades, or even enter them manually. Figure out what works systematically; then divide and conquer.

Dos of Coteaching:

- Make each other a priority.
- Listen to each other.
- Plan lessons at least a week in advance. (You will most likely have to plan farther ahead when working with someone else.)
- Use each other's strengths in the classroom.
- Be honest and always do what's best for the class.
- Put your egos aside.
- Know each other's sensitivity levels.
- Use every adult in the room as a teacher or distributer of knowledge.

- Split the behind-the-scenes classwork and preparation.

- Settle frustrations behind closed doors as soon as possible with honesty and empathy to be able to move past the issue. Compromise if needed.

- Praise each other for what part of the lesson each did well daily or weekly.

- Thank each other weekly or daily.

- Write each other handwritten thank-you cards every once in a while.

- Be open to learning from one another.

- Let each other flop, in front of the class. That's how each will learn.

Don'ts of Coteaching:

- Argue or have a disagreement about the lesson out loud in front of the students. Don't debate about what to do or what not to do. Remember that if you're planning together, you are already both on the same page. Students do not need to see or hear disagreements or lack of planning. There can be a few circumstances where you flow fabulously together, or your lessons have the same basic structure. It's like you do the same dance. However, it's more fun for the students and more beneficial to the learning if you switch it up once in a while and change teaching roles in the classroom.

- Try to wing it. On top of just being bad teaching, it will be a train wreck with more than one person in the room.

- Use one of the adults as the disciplinarian and the other as the teacher.

- Vent to another in your workplace about how frustrated you are with your coteacher.

- Hold in your frustrations and refuse to address them. They *will* come out eventually, one way or another.

- Talk over each other in the lesson. Know your parts.

- Correct each other in front of the class. If correction is needed, pass a note or whisper into an ear. Every teacher makes mistakes. Correcting a teacher in front of the class can be the single most undermining act to a teacher, not to mention very embarrassing. Okay, if you have a really solid relationship with the person, and you've discussed it privately, it can be done in a light-hearted and tasteful manner, sometimes. In five years of coteaching, there

(Continued)

(Continued)

was only one coteacher I could do that with once in a while. After the lesson, I asked her if it offended her when I chimed in. Be very careful with this. This is one of the main reasons coteachers become frustrated. The class will also lose trust that the teacher knows what she is talking about. Be respectful to each other and don't put the mistake on display for everyone. Think of parents who are always waiting for their child to mess up. This is how you will make your coteacher feel. If you have a strong respect for each other and have been working together a while (this usually makes a difference), there are a few exceptions where adding another point of view could build confidence and show students there may be two ways to achieve the same goal. Doing this can also confuse students with lower skill sets. Be careful!

You'll find with one person one way works, and with another a different way may work. I used to work with one woman who was so different from me we would joke back and forth in front of the class. The students loved it. Another woman and I had a large difference in age, so she played the loving grandmother to the students, and that worked. Another time, there were three of us in a powerful triad and we played good cop, bad cop, and middleman. It was equally powerful. Do what works for both of you, make sure you are both heard and respected in the classroom, and make sure having two teachers in the classroom accelerates the learning. Do not use a coteacher solely to discipline. That makes for an unhealthy learning environment.

Your turn

1. Whether you coteach now or not, chances are almost guaranteed that you will work with another adult in the room at some point in your teaching life. Think back to a time when you did not see eye to eye with another adult in the room. How did you handle the situation?

   _____

   _____

   _____

   _____

   _____

   _____

2. If you could have a redo, is there a way you could have improved that specific situation?

   _____

   _____

   _____

   _____

   _____

   _____

Be a Sponge

Teaching is one of those rare professions where it is okay to use other people's ideas, with permission of course. As teachers, we too often reinvent the wheel. Be smart about your time and energy. Don't be afraid to ask your peers for what you need. Ask your fellow teachers if you may have copies of their worksheets. Some teachers will go so far as to write their name on the bottom as a copyright for their hard work. As a sign of respect, keep those names on the worksheets to give credit where credit is deserved. Do not be afraid to ask knowledgeable teachers for their opinions on what to do on a lesson. Share resources whenever you can.

The reality, unless you are that one person who is the best teacher in the world, is this: There is someone who is better than you out there. Lots exist, actually. Many are better than I, and I love when I find them. Or, perhaps they are better at one aspect of teaching. Learn from those educators, and use what works with your style. Remember that you want to create the best you in the classroom.

I remember a day the vice principal came in to my eighth-grade classroom to observe. After the lesson, he asked me how I knew that all students understood the lesson. I admitted that I was not sure. He suggested that I have the students do a thumb check. After I explained a concept to the class, I would ask to see their thumbs. If they understood and were ready to work on their own, they would give me thumbs up. If they did not understand, they would give me a thumbs down, and I would pull those students into a group to go over the concept again. If they were not sure how well they knew the concept, they would give me a sideways thumb, and I would perhaps pull these students into the thumbs-down group as well. You know I still use that tactic to this day with my high school students?

Sharing ideas not only makes you a better teacher, but makes the person sharing knowledge feel appreciated. You can even go beyond your school and Google to look for teaching ideas: Join an online network of teachers on a blog or even perhaps a Meetup group in your area. Successful teaching strategies that work are everywhere. I often get my best ideas from my nonteacher friends. A fresh and nonbiased perspective is priceless. Everyone you know went to school at some point, and they likely have great ideas and input. They will probably give you ideas about what they wished their teachers had done or what their favorite teachers did.

Your turn

1. In your opinion, why is it important to learn to ask for help with ideas when you are a teacher?

   _____

   _____

   _____

   _____

   _____

2. When is the last time you asked someone for ideas for a lesson? Did it help or not?

   _____

   _____

   _____

   _____

   _____

3. Think of a lesson you are planning for the near future. How could a fresh perspective help you? Think of one person you can ask for ideas in the next week.

   _____

   _____

   _____

   _____

   _____

BEST PRACTICE #33

Find a Mentor

Luckily, I never had to find a mentor because my mentor found me. In my third year of teaching our school psychologist was looking for a classroom to coteach in to gather research for her PhD dissertation. I was approached with the idea and was immediately self-conscious about someone else being in my classroom. I first wondered why I was chosen. Did I need help? Was there something wrong with the way I was teaching? Then I became territorial because of all of the hard work I had already dedicated to my class. I had a rhythm that I did not want to break.

To say our first meeting was a train wreck would be an understatement. I was my stubborn self, not wanting any help I didn't ask for, and our school psychologist was frustrated. Little did I know that the woman who I thought was trying to barge into my classroom would be my mentor for many years after. The engagement and smiles she brought to the class were a sight to be seen. The secret about choosing the most beneficial mentor is that your mentor has to be better than you at teaching. I knew I needed her in my life to become a better teacher.

As teachers, we can acknowledge that the most powerful learning for students is one-on-one instruction. This works the same for teacher education. If you want to learn fast, I suggest you find your teaching "guru." Whom you choose as your guru is a very personal decision. The issue is that many teachers don't have the time to sit down and teach another person.

Here's what you can do. Find the teachers that you want to be like one day—shoot for the stars. If you could be the teacher of your dreams, which ones would you emulate? Now, watch them. Visit their classrooms and take notes. Listen to how they speak with students. Ask if you may have a copy of their lesson plans to try out with your students. Learn how they think. Depending on how willing they are to help you on your teacher journey, they may even be able to sit down with you and go over your plans each week. Make the time to learn from them. Although I've had one significant mentor in my life, each year I choose a different person to learn from. Whom I choose depends on where I am in my career.

I remember watching my mentor teacher teach a group of eighth graders. She would gather all of the students to take notes and introduce a concept as they were sitting in a close circle around her. She had their full attention. But instead of standing, she would sit at their level in a chair or sometimes even on the floor, even with middle school students. This had an amazing effect on the students. They were calm and focused. They didn't feel threatened or talked down to. They were learning with the teacher. I used this strategy with my classes. With a few classes, I even had the students sitting on chairs while I sat cross-legged on the floor while teaching. This method seemed to calm my students while also empowering them. This also gives the teacher the chance to relate to students on their level. I've observed identical results with every group of students I've taught in that manner.

Imitating a few key tactics from your mentor will draw you out of your comfort zone or give you new ideas and stretch you to become the teacher you want to be. Eventually, you will incorporate these techniques in future lessons without your mentor's help, but in the meantime, learning directly from someone else will push you to where you need to be.

I worked with my guru for three entire years before I felt I could work on my own at the level I wanted to teach. She was my Mr. Miagi of teaching and seemed to know all of the strategies and secrets. Although I did not need her as much anymore, I still e-mailed her from time to time with a question or two. The secret was that I never called her "my mentor," because I didn't want to scare her away. I'm sure she knew that she was acting as one, but because I never called her one, we formed a friendship out of choice rather than obligation. I've been told that the word *mentor* scares people, because it suggests that they will be obliged to put a lot of time and energy into you. Good luck finding the teachers of your dreams and emulating them! You'll find you will not need them one day and will blossom into your fullest self as a teacher, but you will appreciate and grow from their help in the beginning.

Your turn

1. Think of a teacher in your life whom you admire. What is it about this person's teaching that appeals to you? Do you see these qualities in yourself?

_____

_____

_____

_____

_____

_____

_____

_____

2. How can you learn from this person without taking up large amounts of precious time?

_____

_____

_____

_____

_____

_____

_____

_____

Best Practice #34

Watch and Learn

. . . .

I have always been a visual learner. I learn most effectively by watching. To improve as a teacher, I *had* to see better teaching. During my second year of teaching, our school did not have an observation program. This didn't stop me. I would walk up and down the hallways and basically spy on other classes. I wanted to see which teachers I could learn from. Eventually, I decided to take a more traditional approach and ask teachers if I could come in and observe their classes, instead of just pushing my face against the door window or peeking in through the crack in the classroom door for a few minutes until I was spotted by an alarmed student.

When I found a style I liked, or an appealing way a teacher spoke, or a teacher with a grace about her, or most important a classroom full of engaged students sharing (keep in mind that well behaved and engaged are not necessarily the same thing—I never thought a classroom that silenced children was inspiring to anybody), I would ask that teacher if I could come and observe.

Always ask for permission first; very few teachers will say no, and quite honestly, you probably do not want to learn from a person who doesn't want you to visit. Let the teacher know that you've heard great things about his teaching and that you would like to come by one period to observe. This will give you an immediate positive rapport with another adult and should give you an open door to that classroom. Sit in on a class or two, take notes, and try the same moves in your classroom that you see on your visit.

It's especially powerful to watch classes that teachers may have trouble with, as well as classes they brag about. This will give you a well-rounded idea of the teacher as a whole and give you ideas on how to redirect students effectively if you need to.

Your turn

1. How many times have you taken the time to watch another teacher you
   admire in the past few months? If you have not done this, when is a specific
   time you could watch another teacher? How will you make this happen?

   _____

   _____

   _____

   _____

   _____

2. What did you learn from watching that teacher? Can you name one or two
   specifics that you can use to improve your teaching?

   _____

   _____

   _____

   _____

   _____

BEST PRACTICE #35

Instead of Talking, Listen With Your Mind

. . . .

> When you talk, you are only repeating what you already know. But if you listen, you may learn something new.
>
> —Dalai Lama XIV

Teachers are notorious for being the worst audiences. We just are. We are avid learners, but we do a lot of talking about what we already do in the classroom. I'm guilty. Hey, it's not our fault; we are used to having a captive audience every day. We love to talk, tell stories, and feed others with our knowledge. It is the reason many of us entered this noble profession. However, when it comes to becoming a better instructor, you need to hold back and listen when conversing with other teachers. Nine times out of ten, if you sit at a table of educators, I can tell you what is going on.

Let's see. Each teacher tells a story about a student, a lesson, what went well, what was humorous, and what completely flopped. Listen to what *they* did well and what worked. Sitting with a group of teachers reminds me sometimes of sitting with my ninety-three-year-old grandfather and his friends telling war stories or stories of their grandchildren. Oh, how their faces light up as they talk about themselves, similar to how a teachers' faces light up as they talk about their classes.

Work to listen to these stories of students, tactics, and tricks. Listen during lunch, before and after meetings, and during hallway conversation. Take mental notes. Listen with your mind. We have to remember to think: *How can I use what I am hearing, or not use what I am hearing?* I'm not saying to whip out a notepad and take notes during casual conversation, although that would be humorous. What could you use from these stories in your own classroom? What do you never want to do? Is a teacher telling about something the students loved? Try it. Ask questions and get more specifics. This is free, fast, and real knowledge being given to you. Take it and use it.

Your turn

1. Think of the last time you had a conversation with another teacher about his classroom. Jot down what the conversation was about.

   _____

   _____

   _____

   _____

   _____

2. Did you use that conversation to listen with your mind? What could you have done differently to turn the conversation into a learning experience for you?

   _____

   _____

   _____

   _____

   _____

3. When was the last time you learned something valuable and transferable to your classroom from talking to another teacher? What did you learn?

   _____

   _____

   _____

   _____

   _____

**BEST
PRACTICE
#36**

Be Proactive:
Get and Keep
Administration
on Your Side

This section is one of the longest in the book because it's one of the most important. You have the power to make your administration or school leadership team your best friends or your worst enemies. They can be your biggest help or your biggest obstacle. Your relationship with your administration will directly affect your job satisfaction.

The happiest teachers usually have a great relationship with their administration and feel supported. Honestly, I've been on both sides. I'll say my teaching life was one hundred times more pleasant and easier when my school leadership was on my side. When I worked in charter schools, I had to stay friendly with administration to succeed, since charter schools have the freedom to hire and keep the specific teachers they want and need year after year (and I was lucky to have supportive administration, so this was natural). I did not have a union and actually preferred it that way, since I worked hard, kept a growth mindset, and produced results. I wanted merit to be a factor in my job security and mobility, not just seniority. When I worked for other (non charter) public schools, I still found that administration wanted to be invited into the classroom, even though they didn't necessarily get to hand pick their teachers every year. In either case, it's powerful for the kids to have administration supporting what they are doing and learning.

Tips for Earning the Respect of the Administration

- Invite administrators to student presentations—let them see your students at their best.
- Maintain positive relationships with students as well as their parents.
- Lead an extracurricular group or club.
- Attend school sporting or extracurricular events.
- Coach a sports team.
- Volunteer to help chaperone field trips.
- Invite administration to your room to participate in an engaging learning activity (more details below).
- Give thank-you cards to administration at the end of every school year.
- Show up to work consistently and on time. Respect the work-year calendar.
- Host parent nights and other events that include parents in your classroom.
- Speak about your students respectfully. (Administration will hear your tone.)
- Respect the infrastructure of the school. (If you have an issue with a student, parent, or colleague, go to your direct supervisor first, instead of over the supervisor's head to administration, which can cause more problems for administration in the long run.)

When we teach, we're a part of the web of communication that makes up a school. Often, due to lack of time, our interactions with our administrators are quick: "Hey, how are you?" "Great, thanks," in passing to the restroom or to the office to check our mailbox. Many times, administrators want to know about the great things going on in our classroom, but we just never get the time or opportunity to tell them about it.

There are times during the year that we may need some support, and frankly, even some "favors" from administration. I remember a time when I needed a form signed faster than the system would allow. A few of my colleagues and I were doing a ninth–grade, problem-based, interdisciplinary unit around endangered species. Students chose an endangered species in their science class, developed and researched questions in their English class, and composed a presentation and elegant solution to save the species. They actually built a geometric biome in their geometry class. Our physical education teachers also got on board, and they did teambuilding games around the different species.

One of our teachers heard that the local zoo had free tickets for students on field trips. This was perfect! The problem was that we needed to arrange transportation, and fast. We had about a day to make it happen. However, getting bus transportation required many forms, signatures, and e-mails, each of which could take a day or two. We were stuck in "the system."

It may feel like administrators sit in the office all day making phone calls, taking extended lunches, and joking with their colleagues while sipping espressos. Although a part of me does think that they do that just once in a while, many times they are dealing with scheduling, policies, and regulations that affect the school at large; financial issues; very angry parents; extreme discipline issues; and budget constraints (just to name a few). The truth is that they do care, but they're a little removed from the everyday success that we are fortunate enough to see as teachers. In all honesty, they miss it a little. Remember, most administrators started out as teachers.

So, here's my point. To navigate your way around the system and cash in your favor points to get around systematic roadblocks, you have to start early.

You see, I had a lot of points in my bag I had been saving up for years. You will, too. Here is my best advice to get them.

1. **Let your students speak louder than you do.**

Let's say your students do a really impressive project or problem-based learning unit. This usually happens around the middle to the end of the year. Usually at the end of a project there is a day when the students show off what they did. Perhaps it's a gallery walk, or a group presentation, or a demonstration. So, the day you have your presentations and students show off their work, do you ever invite administration in?

When I do this, I usually have the class vote to see if they want visitors. (They'll always say yes if their proud of their work.) I have someone in the class (with really nice handwriting) compose an invitation. You may need to talk the class into this with your best salesperson skills, but once the class votes to have administration invited, they will work twice as hard on their projects.

Next, instead of asking administration yourself, choose two to four students from each class who are outspoken and really proud of their projects to deliver the invitations. Students who are proud of their work will advertise the project the best. Have them hand-deliver an invitation to each person in administration. Coach them on what to say and what to do if they see the administrator talking to another teacher, and have them practice with you a few times. This is also teaching socioemotional skills any student can use in life.

It's extra helpful if you can include a student who is constantly in trouble be one of the deliverers of the invitation. Also, if you choose one of these students to deliver the invitation, it may spark some motivation to work harder on the project in the days leading up to the presentation. *Remember: Students who often get into trouble for "talking at inappropriate times" usually have advanced interpersonal skills.* Use this strength, and choose this student to be one of the ones to hand-deliver the invitation. There are a few reasons for this:

a. Selecting this student as one of the class representatives to deliver the invitations will help build self-esteem and a positive self-image for this student. This could lead to stronger self-management and motivation in your class for the rest of the year. Hopefully, this positive self-image will also spread to other parts of the student's life. When these students know that the whole class is waiting for them to get that invitation delivered, they will not goof around. Trust me.

b. Administration wants to see these students succeed. You are showing administration that you are reaching the "unreachable" students in your classroom. In turn, you are indirectly advocating for yourself in a very loud way without having to say a word.

I usually also send an e-mail to administration listing what they will be seeing, how it is linked to the standards, what we did to lead up to the learning, what the unit was about, et cetera. In other words, I send them the "adult talk." Having administration show up and be impressed with your students is really powerful for the students.

2. **Have students lead displays of learning at the end of a project.**

It's especially powerful if you can have administration see a student-led display of learning. This shows you can empower students. It includes but is not limited to the following:

1. Student greeters at the door (especially if parents are also coming). Teach them how to stand, what to say, how to smile, et cetera.

2. Student seaters (if visitors are to sit).

3. Students saying opening words and closing words (if it is a performance).

4. Student translators (if many of the parents speak a language other than English) in opening and closing. Have the student translators practice the translation before the day of the performance. You'll find some students are much better at translating than others. Many times two students can split the translation task and alternate.

Around my fifth year of teaching, I managed to have displays or even performances of learning where I could sit back and just watch. The students did everything. If you can work up to this in your first few years of teaching, administration will notice, and most important, your students will see how much you believe in them to let them lead. They will notice the smiles, et cetera, and feel like their work was "worth watching." Usually, after administration comes, students like to share with each other the reactions of each administrator. "Did you see how Dr. Gary was smiling ear to ear? He even said to me. . . ." They'll have stories like this.

Administrators often have last-minute meetings and obligations, so it's always a gamble whether or not they can make it. Let your students know this. However, even if administrators can't attend the presentation, in their minds you are already the teacher who inspired that student who constantly gets into trouble. Also, they are able to gauge the excitement in your students' voices during the brief interaction with the invitation delivery. Last, administrators will see that you taught students how to code switch and formally interact with adults, which is an important life skill. Administration will start to notice you and might just remember how excited your students were for their project when you find yourself stuck in the system and need a form signed fast. Students can advocate for your classroom much better than you can.

3. **Write thank-you cards.**

You always want to keep yourself on good terms with people who hold the system in place. Give your administrators, department head, administrative assistants, school nurse, coteachers, and custodian a handwritten thank-you letter around holiday time or at the end of every school year. These are people who help make your classroom happen. A thank-you card is a simple and quick way to do this. You could also write a quick e-mail, but a handwritten thank-you note is timeless and appreciated.

4. **Be proactive.**

My mentor once told me that having a supportive administration is almost as important as the type of students at a school, if not more so. Some of the lowest-performing schools have some of the happiest teachers due to administrative support. Being proactive is the most effective way to find a supportive administration. Now, with social media, it's easy to find someone who knows someone who works at a district or school you are interested in. Try your hardest to get a chance to chat with that person on the phone. Ask about administrative support specifically. If you can find two people who work for a district or school, even better. See if their answers are consistent. LinkedIn is a great way to find a connection in a school district. You can also use Facebook or other social media tools to ask.

The fact is, in my experience, if people know what you're doing in the classroom, and like what you are doing in the classroom, and see that you're making an effort, the system is easier to work with. People may do things for you faster—if even just a bit faster.

I'm not saying that having a bank of points was the reason I was able to get the field trip documents signed by all of required parties in just a fraction of the time it should have taken, but I think it helped. Administration knew if I was asking for something, it must benefit the kids greatly, because they saw my work in the classroom and trusted my intentions. Save up your points; you'll need them one day.

Your turn

1. How does your administration support you?

_____

_____

_____

_____

_____

2. How could you use the support of your administration to benefit the learning in your classroom?

_____

_____

_____

_____

_____

3. Think of your next class project. Could you invite any of your administration in to participate in the presentations, et cetera? How could this benefit the students?

_____

_____

_____

_____

_____

Real Conversation With Eighth-Grade Students

I only had a few minutes to do grades for the week, and was desperately trying to save some time. I called all students up to my desk who had earned an A that week. All ten stellar students gathered around with their eyes wide and ears perked. I wanted to whisper so the others didn't hear and get jealous. I lowered my head, so the others wouldn't hear, and a sly grin spread across my face.

Me (to the ten students gathered around my desk): You *all* have A's. [I smile.]

Student standing closest to me: What? We all have AIDS?!? [All other students then look up; confusion and some panic starts.]

Me: No, I said A's, A's!

PART 5

SPINS THAT WILL WOW YOUR STUDENTS

We Don't All Have To Be Magicians

I remember way back in my sophomore year of high school I had a really great substitute teacher, Mr. Lombard. He liked to open the class with magic tricks before Spanish class. There was one trick where he had a ghost made of tissue paper and he made it disappear into a cloud of smoke. My Spanish teacher was out on maternity leave pretty early for the first half of the school year so we had him for a couple of weeks. It was awesome!

—Derik, age 34

What do spins that set you apart have to do with classroom management?

How do you want your students to remember you? Depending on the grade, by the time the students have you as a teacher, they've seen it all. They've had strict teachers, they've had fun teachers, they've had boring teachers, and they've had passionate teachers. But they haven't had one type of teacher just yet: you. We certainly do not need to do magic tricks before every class to set ourselves apart, but if we're moonlighting magicians, we should bring that into the classroom to set us apart. Part V includes a few ideas you can use to set yourself apart and stand out. These are types of ways to stand out that kids recognize and enjoy. When you stand out, they enjoy your class, and in turn, students are more inclined to behave and be engaged in the learning.

I REMEMBER WHEN. . . .

I remember when I came across a "Dear Abby" column where a reader told the story of running into an honor student working in a grocery store over the summer. Attempting to ring up gravy packages on sale at four for a dollar, the student proceeded to charge each packet at forty-four cents, commenting, "That's four for a dollar, right?"

As an educator in my tenth year of teaching, the honor student's need for practical application of classroom work resonated with me. Too often, my students could solve a problem on a worksheet or in a classroom setting, but not transfer the skill to a real-world application. This need was even more obvious with my group of third to fifth graders in a self-contained special education class in rural Lumber Bridge, North Carolina. Society seems to have lowered expectations for students with disabilities who are additionally economically disadvantaged, even if they have sympathy and compassion for these students.

But why should this define my students and their future? I frequently submit grant requests for field trips or guest speakers to allow us to maximize opportunities to transfer skills. In 2014 we obtained a class pet from Pets in the Classroom. Striving to maximize this learning opportunity, I e-mailed a local veterinarian, who came to answer questions and discuss proper handling of and care for our hamster. We also reached out to a college, hoping that a vet-tech student could come speak to the class. The college responded, noting that they could send a "VP of Academic Affairs in the Department of Animal Science." As I shared the e-mail aloud and explain that a VP is a vice president, a student's eyes grew wide and his hand shot into the air as he asked, "Ms. Kellermann, did you just say the *president* is coming?"

His peer quickly followed, "Oh I know him, that's Barack Obama." Who knew that a tiny hamster could inspire dialogue beyond pet care? This pint-sized pet led us to a wealth of questions and thinking.

Years later, while completing a short-term Distinguished Awards in Teaching Fulbright fellowship in Botswana, Africa, during the summer of 2017, I was reminded yet again of how integral it is for students to see and apply lessons beyond the four walls of the classroom. My students, a group of young adults between the ages of eighteen and twenty-four, could count *thebe* and *pula* (Botswana currency), yet their understanding was fully realized only once we incorporated these lessons into a training program where they sold oranges from a roadside stand. Now, money had meaning attached to it—a purpose, an exchange of goods—and my students had renewed motivation.

A phenomenal teacher can devise a new idea to implement, but sometimes having a different voice deliver it brings novelty to the situation. Make an effort to extend learning beyond the classroom by inviting in guest speakers. They can be found anywhere—from professionals at local churches to business owners at local establishments. Let them speak to successes and failures. Let them share the challenges to be overcome and the rewards that come from success or failure. Let them see the inner workings that bring childhood passions into employment realities. People love what they do and are willing to share it to inspire others, if we only step outside our normal routines and invite them to WOW our students.

—Jessica Kellermann
Special Education Teacher
11 years' experience
Sandy Grove Elementary
Raeford, North Carolina

BEST PRACTICE #37

Get Guest Speakers Into Your Classroom

To a beginning teacher, having a guest speaker in the classroom may seem like a nightmare waiting to happen. *What if the kids aren't good? What if they say something embarrassing? What if Johnny is having a bad day again?* I completely get it. My second year teaching, my neighboring math teacher invited a guest speaker into his classroom. We had the same group of students. When he told me he was bringing in a guest speaker about a career path they could take, I admired his courage. Our shared group of students was, to put it politely, challenging. He seemed excited and beamed as he was speaking of the speaker. After the event, he came to me furious at the students. He told me of how they were unengaged and rude, and how one student threw a paper ball across the room. That scared me away from guest speakers for a while, until I figured out how to do it.

To be honest, I was lucky to get some help in the beginning from another teacher. She taught me that having a guest speaker can be one of the most powerful learning experiences if you carefully plan, know how to engage the students, and stimulate interaction between the students and the speaker. She showed me that if you choose guests speakers based on the curriculum, and schedule them so the timing aligns with what your students are currently learning or adds a different perspective, and if you can get the students excited about the guest, it makes all the difference. She gave me the courage to try one, which soon turned into many. The results were amazing and I've been hooked ever since. I can give you a few pointers, but each guest speaker is different.

I'm going to share my guest-speaking success stories. I've never had an unpleasant experience, and all have exceeded my expectations. Here are some guests we've had in the classroom over the years who helped bring our units to life:

- civil rights panel

- career interview panel

- retired judge

- Holocaust Auschwitz survivor (via Skype)

- potential astronaut

- music therapist

- art therapist

- family doctor

We also invited a different Holocaust survivor to physically come in to speak during a unit where we read *Night* by Elie Wiesel. However, she was the daughter of a German soldier. At first, my class was very against me inviting her in. A few of the students booed after I explained who she was. I spoke (not lectured) about what she might be feeling, and how she was a little timid to tell me her background. We discussed our different opinions about whether her story was worth hearing. I asked them, in a calm voice, to put themselves in her shoes. They listened.

It just so happened she was frightened and elderly. My students understood this. Her daughter wrote me an e-mail about how her mother was having second thoughts about coming in. Her story was so too personal to her, and she was scared about the reaction of the class knowing the book they were reading. She was afraid nobody would want to hear it or understand it, or worse: They would have an adverse reaction. I could feel her about to back out. I shared this with my classroom. We had a class discussion about what to do. A student suggested we reach out to her. We decided to create a huge poster sign about how excited we were to meet her and to have her come in and speak. The students wrote her quick letters about how much they wanted to hear what she had to say.

This was a game changer. After she got the poster and letters, her daughter e-mailed me and said that the student letters were hanging above her ninety-year-old mother's bed. Her daughter told me that her mother had told her that now she felt like somebody wanted to hear her story. I read the response to my class. I printed out the e-mail and hung it on the wall. The students grew more and more excited as the day of our guest speaker's visit approached.

Tips for Hosting Guest Speakers

- **Prepare the students to welcome the guest speaker.** I did some background work with my class: We constructed a graphic organizer relevant to this guest speaker. The students knew exactly who the visitor was. We also hung up a picture of the visitor in class, so students could identify a face with a name and felt empowered when the guest arrived.

- **Share the story.** Be completely honest with your classroom about the conversation you had with person about coming in. Let them know how it happened! I show the actual e-mails on my document camera, describe the conversations, and play the voicemails on speaker phone for them to hear. The students love hearing that people want to come in and speak to them. This also lets them know that you are talking about them to people in your life. If there is an e-mail chain going back and forth, I show the whole chain. We talk about the thread, how the person must be feeling about coming in, and how we should prepare. This teaches emotional intelligence to our students. It's real. We have a great time looking at it, and they can see the process I used to get someone to come in.

- **Be just a little more excited than your students.** They may not get it at first, but they will. If they're not excited, they most likely just don't understand the full picture. Explain it to them. I was teaching friendly letter writing to my eighth graders one semester, and I decided to give my students a real audience and write letters of gratitude to the local firefighters who worked to put out the wildfires around San Diego County. I was also showing them the power of a thank-you, and also teaching my students about empathy—the fires didn't directly affect them, but they should still care about and appreciate what these firefighters did to save many lives. When we first wrote the thank-you letters, my students didn't believe the letters would ever be read. The response I got from students was, "They'll probably just throw them away. Don't waste money on stamps."

"They won't," I replied. "I think they'll at least hang them on the bulletin board in their snack room. Adults love that stuff."

"Yeah," the kids replied. "That'd be cool," and they kept writing. I was just a little more excited than they were.

A few weeks later, I received a voicemail from the secretary of the fire chief of San Diego asking if he and a few trucks of firefighters could come to our class to say thank-you for the letters. I played the voicemail to my students. They were speechless. A week later, fire trucks pulled into our school parking lot, sirens blazing (my students requested this), along with multiple local news reporters who had heard of this beautiful story of appreciation. My students were all over the local news channels that evening.

The point of this is that I stayed more excited than my students about the letters and sending them to a real audience. The firefighters' visit turned into a beautiful impromptu guest speaking experience for the students to show the power of gratitude. When you stay just a bit more excited than your students, wonderful things will happen for your classroom.

- **Send a letter or card to guest speakers telling them how excited the students are to meet them.** This will help speakers if they feel anxiety, and will help them understand where students are coming from. Teenagers can be scary for speakers! The speaker will come in feeling more warmly about your students.

- **Prepare your students mentally and behaviorally.** I will not discipline my students in front of a guest speaker. I let them know verbally that I will not discipline them and that I trust that they'll represent themselves with respect. I want to empower them so they have as much interaction with the speaker as possible. I prepare them so they know how to greet the speaker, how formal to be, and what to do if the speaker gets nervous. We talk about the signals they send with their body language, what questions they can ask, and what questions they probably should not ask. We have a practice conversation beforehand where students ask me what they really want to know, and I speak to them about how those questions may make the speaker feel and how to reword them if needed. My students interact with the guest speakers and know they can ask the difficult questions, because I've taught them how to word the questions tactfully. These are the powerful moments to watch.

- **Trust your students to take ownership.** The students see me taking myself out of the equation and they understand that I trust them. We prepare about two weeks in advance. If you set expectations, do not threaten, and do a thorough job letting the students know why the speaker wants to come in, the kids will rise to the occasion. Every speaker I've had in my classroom has left with a powerful experience. And what's more, the students took ownership. I never have my students come in and just take notes. They can do that with a video. If there's a live person in the room, it's essential to teach them how to interact and how to ask the right questions. That is when the true learning happens.

In a room filled with 125 inner-city eighth graders, you could have heard a pin drop as this woman in a wheelchair told her story. She spoke about the love she had for her father and what she remembered from her youth. I had my students write their questions first on sticky notes and hand them to me. I wouldn't normally do this, but because of the fragility of the speaker and the emotional vulnerability of her topic, I looked at the questions first. (Otherwise, I urge you to let you students ask their own questions.) The main purpose of inviting this guest speaker was to show the students that as they go out into the world, there will be conflicts where people will feel love on both sides. It's important to listen to what people have to say, because everybody has a story worth hearing.

Your turn

1. What types of guest speakers would tie into your upcoming units to accentuate learning?

_____

_____

_____

_____

_____

2. What message does inviting guest speakers into the classroom give to your students?

_____

_____

_____

_____

_____

3. What is the importance of having guest speakers in your classroom?

_____

_____

_____

_____

_____

BEST PRACTICE #38

Give Students Power and a Voice

· ·

In this class we share our thoughts, comments, opinions because we *all* have something important to say.

—Sara, Grade 8

One of the most difficult skills for teachers to master is how to give students power and still keep control. It goes against our natural instinct as a teacher, but it is rich in benefits.

Tips for Giving Students Power (and Still Keeping Control)

- **Give students a structured forum to converse with one another, and be a strong facilitator.**

  Example: Have sentence starters for student discourse (to agree and respectfully disagree) visible at all times for students to use in class or group academic conversations.

  Nonexample: Scold students for disagreeing heatedly in academic discourse without offering redirection.

  (Continued)

(Continued)

- **Allow students to vote on decisions that do not impede learning.** Keep in mind that sometimes you do know best.

  Example: Students vote on whether you have a class lead librarian, or everyone helps manage the class library.

  Nonexample: Students vote on whether or not to do the lesson that day.

- **Incorporate student choice into your lessons.**

  Example: Students get to choose their own group leaders within their group of four students, or students get to choose which short story they want to write an essay about from a choice of four stories.

  Nonexample: Students choose which students work in the group to finish a task, and which students do not.

- **Have student leaders in activities.**

  Example: Have a student keep score during a class activity.

  Nonexample: Let one student boss around an entire group.

- **Use students as teachers in small groups**

  Example: Use the student who scored highest on the test to reteach a concept to a small group of students who did not do well on the same test in her own way.

  Nonexample: Use the loudest student, who may or may not fully understand the concept, as the group leader only because other students listen to him.

- **Let students voice their opinion.** Make sure the squeaky wheels don't have the loudest voice. Let them know there is a time and a place for any opinion to be expressed.

  Example: Allow students to ask you to slow down if you are teaching too fast for them to learn. Thank them for expressing their learning needs.

  Nonexample: Allow a class venting session where students all complain about why they shouldn't have to learn a concept. Beware of classroom mob mentality. If this happens, tell them you are sorry they feel this way, but they need to understand this concept.

- **Do projects where students can set their own pacing.** Check in often, and make sure to help the struggling students so they feel as successful as other students.

  Example: Assign a project where the students create a timeline of when they will have each part of the project complete.

  Nonexample: Allow students to not do work for one week and rush to finish the project at the last minute. This does not teach time management.

Your turn

1. Discuss a time when either you or a teacher you observed incorporated student choice in a lesson. What did this look like, and how did this affect student engagement?

_____

_____

_____

_____

2. How and when can you give students opportunities to set and monitor their own pacing with a larger assignment or project? How do you monitor students who fall behind or work too quickly? What life skill does this teach students?

_____

_____

_____

_____

3. What are your thoughts on class votes? How would this look in a class? Share an example of when a class vote could be helpful. What message does allowing class votes send to the students?

_____

_____

_____

_____

BEST PRACTICE #39

Show Your Students You Care

You have been the most caring teacher that I have ever had. I have learned a lot in your class, not just about English but about people.

—Luis, Grade 9

One of the most common complaints students have about a teacher is "My teacher doesn't like me." Sounds childish, right? Guess what? Most students are still children. I hear this complaint from middle school students and high school students just as often. Think about it. We, adults, do it too. Think back to your favorite teacher. I am sure you had a strong sense that this teacher enjoyed your company as a human being. Think back to your least favorite teacher. I'm sure you felt disrespected, ignored, or just not liked. My mentor once told me, "Students remember how they felt in your class, not so much what you did."

How do your students feel in your class? Happy? Loved? Scared to mess up? Talked down to? Silenced? Heard? Constantly yelled at? Like a disappointment? Like the smartest students in the world? Don't just tell them you care; *show* them.

Tips for Showing Your Students That You Care About Them

- **Prepare materials for success.** Have tissues and supplies ready to set students up for success. Show them that you are doing everything on your end to help them, and you also care if their nose runs.

- **Talk *to* students.** New teachers almost always talk *at* the class. Experienced teachers talk *to* the students. Listen to the difference.

- **Be firm and caring.** These two characteristics cannot be mutually exclusive. One does not work without the other. If you are too firm, it may seem that you want them to fail. If you are too lenient, they may feel you do not care enough to push them.

I recommend you make exceptions for some students, privately. Tell them you are making the exception for them specifically. Think of the police officer that pulls you over. You were obviously speeding. You plead your case, and he listens and makes an exception. Would you run and tell the DMV how nice the police officer was? Probably not, but you would like that officer. You would see him as empathetic and having a heart. He most likely told you he was going to "let you go with a warning this time." Do the same with a few of your students *once in a while, and privately.* Give secret extensions. Give a student in need a notebook that he may have lost. If you do this, that student will love you! Make sure you use this tool very sparingly. Have the conversation with the student that you are, in fact, making an exception because you want to see him succeed, and do not let the other students see, or you will have a battle on your hands. Care enough to do what the child needs.

- **Give returning students a few minutes.** When the students come back from a break or long weekend, give them a few minutes to catch up with their friends. They are going to do it regardless, so why not structure it? I usually set a timer for four minutes and thirty-five seconds or some odd number like that (just to let them know I am controlling the structure), and I tell them to ask each other how they spent their holiday break. Sometimes they roll their eyes and say, "Wow, thanks." I then admit that that's not a lot of time and jokingly add on another second. That usually gets a laugh. Most times I'll set it up like this:

(Continued)

(Continued)

Teacher: I think I'd like to give you five minutes to talk to your tables about your break. Do you think you'll be able to refocus on the learning today if I give you that time?

Class will always say yes.

Teacher: Let's do this. Tell me right now. If you think you're going to have trouble refocusing after I give you five minutes, could you raise your hand? You're not in trouble; I just need to know who may need a little extra help. [say it with a smile]

Almost always, a couple of students will raise their hands. Basically, they don't want to let the class down, so they're revealing themselves.

Teacher: Okay, great. I will be sure to help you out a bit. Thanks for letting me know. Okay, here we go!

Start the timer, project the time, and let kids socialize. You can talk to them, too, if you like, at their desks. Look out for students sitting alone and not talking to anybody. When you see this, discreetly ask a kind student in the class to go over and ask them about their break. This is also a great opportunity to have students feel like they belong. It's a good idea to project the time on the document camera so they can *see* how much time they have to talk, and in case a supervisor walks in and wonders what is going on. It's a structured social time, so you can get right back into learning after the five minutes. Five minutes will earn you lots of respect. When you stop the timer, they should be back in their seats and extra ready for you, since you did them a favor already. The two kids that revealed themselves actually probably won't be an issue or need to be redirected.

You're also building a healthy community here when students are getting to know one another in an unstructured setting and "unclogging" anything they just have to get out of their brains so they can fit learning in. In addition, learning is a social activity, so creating structure for students to build friendships in the classroom will help your academic environment. Also, they will most likely laugh a bit, so they will be lowering their affective filters before they learn. These four minutes and thirty-five seconds will benefit your lesson in many ways.

Now, enjoy your Day 1 of learning after a break. It works. It will seem like you have given them a gift, and your lesson will be much easier.

- **Let students know when they do a good job.** It's that simple. Chances are, unless they have spectacular parents, they already hear all about how they need to do better, be more like their more responsible sibling, or study more. Compliment them when they do a good job, act in a pleasant way, do well on a test, are kind to a classmate, or answered a question with critical thinking. Students will perform more for you when you recognize their strengths. Start small if you have to. Even if you compliment somebody's handwriting, you'll be surprised what effect that can have.

Remember: If you are waiting for students to fail, they will fail. If you are recognizing their strengths, you are helping them succeed. Point out what students do right, not just what they do wrong. They already get enough criticism.

It's easy to show you care when the student is likeable. However, what do you do with those students who just get under your skin and push your buttons? You have to see their *strengths*. Breathe, and think about the students' strengths. This is your job. Learn to respect each student.

Your turn

1. How do you *show* your students that you care? Can you add to the ideas in the previous pages?

_____

_____

_____

_____

2. Do your words and your actions match in the classroom?

_____

_____

_____

_____

3. Is there a student in your classroom that may feel like you don't like her as a person? How can you change this in an authentic way?

_____

_____

_____

_____

BEST PRACTICE #40

Laugh Together and You Will Learn Together

· ·

This is the funniest class I've ever been in.

—Jayden, Grade 8

In my second year teaching, I remember one time when the entire class laughed. I was disciplining the class, big surprise, and the entire class burst out in laughter. They were all looking right at me. I turned red and asked why they were laughing, and then tried to stop them from laughing. This moment may be a teacher's biggest nightmare.

One empathetic student pulled a hand mirror out of her backpack and let me see what was causing the hysterics. I had somehow rubbed blue marker from my hand to my nose. Rudolph the Blue Nosed Reindeer was trying to scold them! They eventually stopped laughing because they felt so bad for me, although some still couldn't stop. I can only imagine how silly I looked with my stern face, disciplining the rowdy class with a bright blue nose. This is the only laughter I remember in my classroom that year.

Now, I laugh with my classes on a daily basis. My students affectionately say my laugh sounds like a dolphin. It actually does.

Do your students know what your laugh sounds like?

Usually, it's in the beginning of class when I let students share any good news they have or let them share interesting stories (for about two minutes), such as Black Friday shopping stories, crazy things their younger brothers and sisters did that weekend, or just funny things they noticed around school. Laughter breaks down barriers, brings people together, and relieves anxiety and stress. Laughing makes students feel safe and helps shy students lose their fear. People don't laugh when they're stressed or anxious. I know if we're laughing, we're relaxed and ready to learn. We laugh now as a class for a specific purpose. They are not afraid to laugh in my class, they know never to laugh directly at someone, and they see me laugh all of the time. We laugh together and we learn together.

Companies are starting to realize this. There is a push in the corporate field, especially with managers and corporate leaders, to utilize laughter to strengthen relationships with coworkers to maximize productivity. Shawn Achor, Harvard teacher and world leading happiness expert, published a book, *The Happiness Advantage* (2010), exploring how happiness is one of the leading factors of performance. He teaches a happiness course to companies worldwide showing corporate leaders how happy workers significantly increase the performance of a company.

> A teacher who can get students to laugh can get students to open up and learn.

Teachers can use this valuable insight as well. A teacher who can get students to laugh can get students to open up and learn.

Tips for Infusing Productive Laughter

- **Have a stuffed class pet.** I always have a different stuffed animal every year that is our pet. Dress it up differently some days, and have it in the front of the class. You want a medium-sized pet, because students will hold it as they are learning some days—nothing too small. I had our class rat (we named him Ratatouille) in a Halloween costume when fall arrived, Santa hat when December approached, and swim gear when it got hot. It always made students chuckle when they came in. The students will notice it immediately and it will be a great opener. Even better yet if the costume can relate to what you are learning. Even my high schoolers loved Mr. Giggles (our stuffed lion). They stopped by my classroom year after year to ask what he was up to.

- **Give humorous surprise prizes.** Why not make some of your classroom prizes or incentives humorous? Add some funny prizes. Have only a few of these, though, or the class won't trust your prizes. A girl in my class once won a mini packet of soy sauce, and her face lit up. The whole class was thrilled. We all had a good laugh together. Make sure the student who wins the prize shows it to the class, so you can all laugh together. You can also give the student a real prize afterward if you wish, depending on your style. You could have a big box with an opening for the student to reach in and pull out a prize. Or, think more creatively and have a fishing rod and a shower curtain. Students "fish" for a prize (you clip something to their line). The point is that the sky is the limit.

- **Tell funny stories.** Tell a funny story about something that happened to you once in a while. Make sure it's a learning experience, so they understand why you are telling it and you're just not the crazy too-much-information teacher. It makes you more human. It is even better if you can weave the appropriate story into the lesson. Be careful that your story is appropriate. I once had a student run back to me to report an off-the-wall story another teacher told him, saying, "Can you believe that story Ms. So-and-So told us?" That makes you seem irresponsible and a bit crazy. I would tell you that story but it's inappropriate for even this book. And please, no sob stories. The students don't need to know all your business.

Your turn

1. Do you agree that laughter can increase learning and productivity in a class-room? Why or why not?

    _____

    _____

    _____

    _____

    _____

    _____

    _____

2. How do your students have fun in class while they are learning? Brainstorm three new ideas!

    _____

    _____

    _____

    _____

    _____

    _____

    _____

    _____

Give Gifts

....

Whether you like it or not, you will probably spend more time with the students in your class than with even your closest friends during the school year. A wise teacher takes advantage of this opportunity to make the student/teacher relationship healthy and positive for both parties. You will spend birthdays and other holidays with the students of your classroom. I always think of my students as part of my extended family, in a sense. Show them you care on these holidays, and there's nothing wrong with a little gift every once in a while. For example, on Valentine's Day, I gave each student a wooden pencil with hearts and "Happy Valentines Day" written on it.

Gifting is also a great way to remind students to say thank-you when receiving a gift. If students did not say, "thank you" when I handed them the pencil, instead of scolding them, I gave them the benefit of the doubt. I said overly loud to the next student, "you're welcome!" and usually the students who forgot would bashfully scream out, "Oh, sorry, thank you, Ms. Pariser!" In return, many students started giving me candy, apples left over from their lunch, et cetera, to show that they cared as well. You're indirectly teaching gratitude and giving just for the sake of giving. Around the winter holidays, I may hand out one Hershey kiss to each student and say "Happy Holidays."

Don't break the bank, but a tiny gift goes a long way—yes, even for high school students. It shows them you care, you are human, you wish them well, and you appreciate them as human beings. If the gift is small, I usually joke about how I spent all the money in my bank account and got all I could afford on my teacher's salary. They appreciate the chuckle and graciously take the piece of candy with a smile. It's a win-win situation. The secret is not to spend so much that you make the students feel guilty or feel like they owe you something. After all, you may be spending your hard-earned money on supplies. Spend the amount of time and money you like (I usually spend five to ten dollars per holiday tops for all the students). A bag of pencils, pens, or a little something goes a long way. As with all gifts, it's the thought that counts. Students do not expect gifts from teachers at school, so you'll look like a hero and show you care.

Your turn

1. Teachers could have varying opinions on gifting. What is your stance?

   _____

   _____

   _____

2. What does gifting tell your students?

   _____

   _____

   _____

3. How could gifting maximize learning in your class?

   _____

   _____

   _____

4. How do you feel when you give someone a gift "just because"?

   _____

   _____

   _____

5. How do you feel when you receive a gift "just because"?

   _____

   _____

   _____

BEST PRACTICE #42

Be the Teacher
They Never Had

Thank you for having me in your class this year. You are by far the best teacher ever. You are my hero. You rescued me from having a very shy and lonely life. You are funny and always give good advice. You have inspired me to be creative and open-minded. A teacher that has that ability to change a fourteen-year-old's life is a very rare gift and I'm very grateful for having a teacher/motivator/ hero in my lifetime. Thank you very much.

—Roy, Grade 9

A student wrote these words to me in my eighth year teaching. I was floored. I had been the teacher he never had because I had given him opportunities to take risks in our classroom. I did this by spending time teaching public speaking with his class in particular. They came to me afraid to make a mistake in the beginning of the year, and very few students would raise their hands or respond when I asked questions. I knew they couldn't be successful in life afraid to speak up. They were soft-spoken, but I could tell they had so much more potential. They needed someone to break them out of their shells and show them that their voices mattered. I did just that.

I don't think you can help students break out of their shells with intimidation or threats. You can't help students break out of their shells by telling them what they are doing wrong over and over again. I also don't think you can help students break out of their shells by maintaining a hostile classroom where students may put each other down at any second. I do know that if you are planning to be the teacher they never had, there are a few fundamentals to establish before anything spectacular can happen.

Tips for Being an Exceptional Teacher

- Create an emotionally safe learning environment from Day 1.

- Give students opportunities to take learning risks, encourage, and move aside. This could look like public speaking, performance, presentations, or Socratic Seminars.

- Be students' #1 fan. Prove this in your actions, tone, and words.

- Let students take risks. Show them it is fine to mess up, and that's how we learn. We have to let students make mistakes without shame or embarrassment. If we don't, they turn into robots that only take small risks to please us. What will this do for them in the long run? They will grow up afraid. You have the opportunity for one year with your students to show them to take big risks, mess up, pick up the pieces, and grow stronger from it. Or, perhaps they do not mess up, and they succeed more than they imagined even in their wildest dreams.

They will leave your room confident and fearless, and you may just have "rescued them from a lonely life."

Your turn

1. How do you react when a student makes a mistake in the classroom? How does this make your students feel about making mistakes?

   _____

   _____

   _____

   _____

2. What is the biggest risk you have ever asked your students to take inside your classroom? Can you brainstorm ways you could have made it bigger?

   _____

   _____

   _____

   _____

3. How do you support students who are afraid to make a mistake?

   _____

   _____

   _____

   _____

Know That Kids Notice the Small Things

We treat this classroom as if we were home.

—Michelle, Grade 8

It's the small things that students notice. A home you love most likely has small loving details, and so should a classroom both you and the class can love. We sometimes do not realize how perceptive students are. I've heard students describe teachers like this, "Oh, Ms. Stanley? She was awesome. She used to have really cool sticky notes."

Tips for Creating a Welcome Classroom Environment

- **Provide tissues and unscented lotion.** I've mentioned tissues before, but it's important enough to mention twice. I'm not sure why, but girls always ask me if I have lotion because their legs or hands are dry. I used to laugh at this and say "of course not," but now I do actually keep an inexpensive small bottle of unscented lotion in a drawer.

(Continued)

(Continued)

- **Put up pictures of students.** Have a spot in your room that is dedicated to pictures of your students working, presenting their work, or just being themselves and having fun. It's important to show both types of pictures. This display shows them you care. Students love taking ownership of the "family board" or "wall of fame." I prefer hard copy pictures hung in the classroom rather than posted on a digital class website: More people can see them, and they can't get passed around on social media. You know what will work best for your students. Let them personalize the display with a child or teenager's touch. Figure 43.1 shows my family board. I also include students' drawings, since art classes are fading fast.

Figure 43.1   Our Family Board

Courtesy of Serena Pariser

- **Keep your classroom clean.** Keeping your classroom clean shows your students you care. Period. It also shows you are a responsible adult. I struggled with this for many years, since I am honestly a naturally messy but mentally organized person. I never missed an appointment but had piles and piles of papers around my room. I had to consciously work to get more organized with *less clutter* for my students. It was difficult. My administrators constantly gently reminded me of what looked messy when they entered my room. (They knew I could take the criticism.) They knew the importance of an organized room for student learning, especially for students who have chaos at home. I was actually appreciative, because I just didn't notice it for some reason. Ask someone else how clean your classroom looks.

Students appreciate and learn better in a clean room. They notice your mess. A messy classroom suggests that you're out of control, and a clean classroom says you have things under control. I now have this under control and make sure the classroom always appears clean and organized. Keeping your classroom under control helps you stay organized and comfortable in your own room. Do you expect your students to have neat and clean habits (neat handwriting, clean backpacks, organized binders)? Then, you should do the same.

- **Keep your classroom up to date.** Students like things new and fresh. It's also extremely healthy for your well-being. Look around the room. Is there a chart or decoration or something written on the board that is outdated? Change it. Take down stale decorations or visuals. If you are hesitant to take down a learning chart or material, make a reference chart that summarizes key concepts from past units, use it when you revisit information, throw away the rest, and move on.

- **Get an air freshener.** Be careful, because kids are particularly sensitive to smell. Nobody can learn in a smelly room, but in my experience everybody always enjoyed the light scent of vanilla.

- **Dress nicely.** Students seem to respect you more when they appreciate your sense of style. They are also fast to criticize it when they do not like a teacher. I'm not saying you have to be dressed for a *Vogue* runway (oh please do not go overboard; this leads to humor, but not respect), but take some time to look put together. Do your hair, put on some mascara, and iron your shirt. Look like you care.

Your turn

1. Think of your classroom aesthetics. How do you show your students that you care? Are there any small details or items you can add to show them you care?

_____

_____

_____

_____

_____

_____

2. What is your opinion of having pictures of students displayed in the class-room? What does this tell the students?

_____

_____

_____

_____

_____

_____

BEST PRACTICE #44

Get Students to Behave When You're Covering Classes

I like your point thingamajig.

—Sarah, Grade 5 (after I covered
her class one day)

I have never been opposed to substitute teaching and don't find the classroom management the hardest part of the job. There is barely any paperwork, the lesson is done for you, if you can't connect with a student you are only there for one or two days, and you can work when you want. What I found most difficult is finding the bathroom in each different school. This is the most frustrating part of substitute teaching for me, not the classroom management. I credit much of my ease with substitute teaching to the subbing classroom management system I developed that I used in every classroom, every subject, every grade. It usually works.

Many people, in fact most teachers I have spoken to, differ. They report that the kids don't behave for someone they do not know. Learning how to effectively cover a class will make your teaching life a lot easier, because the reality is that you will have to cover for your colleagues during your prep (a teacher's free period in the day) some of the time. It's the life of a teacher. Or maybe you're a substitute teacher reading this book.

Here's a trick I use that works ninety-five percent of the time to make your covering-classes life much simpler. Enter class smiling. Students don't take happiness as weakness; in fact they take it as a strength. Your smile will shock them, because they are used to guest teachers coming in with a different affect. If you can go in early, talk to the first student in class (believe me, it won't be the naughty ones who show up first) about anything you're unsure of. They'll answer all questions for you. Do this quietly so you don't get one hundred different answers from other students trying to help.

Then as they come in, get them seated. Say to the class,

"Good morning! My name is Ms/Mr. _____. (Have it written on the board always.) Point to your name. Students will have more respect for you if they know your name. It also shows you have your act together if you have it written before they arrive.

Next, say, "Now, I sub a little differently. You know your teacher better than I do. Think of me as a messenger. I report back one score to your teacher. The score is a whole class score out of 10. Ten is the best. Your current score will always be on the board." Then, write a large 10 on the board, and draw a box around it.

Now say, "You are now at a 10 as a class. If you stay like this, I will report to your teachers that you were a 10-out-of-10 class. However, let's say someone is talking at an inappropriate time or not doing her work. Then it would fall to a 9." Draw a line through the 10 and make it a 9. The class should groan.

"The great thing about this is that you can go up! Once you are on task again, you go right up to a 10!"

The lowest score I've ever reported is a 6, and I've even had classes at 11. You can also give them a list of three criteria they will be graded on. Be sure to write the criteria in behaviors you want to see, not the behaviors you do not want to see. Usually I write these on the side:

You are scored on

1. Following instructions.

2. Respecting your classmates and adults in room with your words and actions.

3. Keeping the noise level at an appropriate volume.

That's it. Write a 10; knock it to a 9, 8, 7 (decrease or increase only one number at a time). Tell them when the number is going up or down. That's it. You should end with between a 7 and a 10 every time. Why does this work?

1. They have a chance to redeem themselves if they mess up.

2. It's not personal. You are not disciplining them individually. Personal disciplining probably won't work with subbing, since you most likely do not have a connection with the students.

3. It uses positive peer pressure. I guarantee you will hear "Sally! Shhh! Quiet! We want our score to go up!"

I've used this from third grade to eleventh grade. By using this method, you're empowering the students. They are taking control of their behavior (they should always be able to see the score), instead of you writing down names of naughty and nice students. It works if you have the expectation that you want them to do well. Try it and see. It's simple and will destress your life when covering classes.

Make sure you report the number to the teacher via e-mail or leave a note at the end of the period or the day. Sometimes classes will compete against each other to see who can get the highest score.

Your turn

1. What are your thoughts on this system? Why do you think it works?

    _____

    _____

    _____

    _____

    _____

2. Does this system empower students, or take away their power?

    _____

    _____

    _____

    _____

    _____

3. What valuable lessons can the students gain using this system?

    _____

    _____

    _____

    _____

    _____

BEST PRACTICE #45

Surprise!

Jill Suttie, in her article, "Why Humans Need Surprise" (2015), points out that surprises increase the amount of dopamine released in our brains, leading to more vitality in our lives. In turn, surprises lead to more vitality in your classroom engagement. We wrap gifts to hide what is inside, and we still have surprise parties. We love getting taken on surprise outings or, for the lucky few, surprise dates. Some of us watch mysteries; others read mystery novels. When life gets too predictable, we get bored. Although structure and consistency are very powerful and work, great teachers know how to intertwine a bit of surprise to keep the spice in their classrooms. As a teacher, I use the element of surprise often. It worked when we were kids; it works when we are adults. Most important, it works with students. It's fun.

Remember: You were hired to create fun, engaging, and rigorous lessons that you sell and deliver to the class. Creating fun lessons with the element of surprise will make your job a bit easier and be more fun for you! When I say surprise, I do not mean balloons have to fall from your ceiling (although, how fun it would be if you could make that happen!). There is a very broad range.

Tips for Adding an Element of the Unexpected to Your Lessons

- **Offer a mystery prize.** If there is a prize for a learning game or activity you have planned, have it out somewhere where the students can see it, but covered. Put a sheet over it, and place a sign over it that says "Mystery Prize" or "What could this be?" Another idea would be

(Continued)

(Continued)

buying one of those fancy covers restaurants put over the plates to keep dishes warm. You could buy one on Amazon or find one in a thrift store and yell "voila!" as you reveal the prize. The point is to make the students wonder. Even if the prize is just a candy bar or a bookmark, the excitement itself makes it a bit more fun for you and them. Just make sure it is not somewhere an impulsive student could prematurely rip off the sheet and wreck your surprise. This is much more exciting than just giving the winner a prize.

- **Let them guess.** Give students two minutes to predict what is in the box under the tray or sheet. You'll be surprised how invigorating these two minutes can be. Be prepared for some really outrageous answers that make you and the class laugh. Laughter brings a classroom together.

- **Create a trail of hints.** Before you read a class novel or start a new unit, make them wonder. Give them little clues each day. Do an activity that hints at what is about to come. You'll find students will start coming up to you in the hallway and trying to guess what the lesson or unit is. Remember the *Of Mice and Men* example I shared in Best Practice #15? This is one solid way to incorporate surprise in your lessons.

- **Pique interest with a prop.** If you plan to use a piece of realia in your lesson, have it out and exposed so the class wonders what you will do with it. Realia are props that help the learning because they link new concepts with a real object. Using realia is a popular strategy for use with English language learners, but it can heighten the learning and increase engagement in any classroom of students. Any real artifact can be a piece of realia. For example, if you are doing a lesson that entails showing the class a project that was completed last year, have that project on display. This will be a focal piece as students walk in the door. Or, if you are teaching Greek mythology and reading the legend of Echo and Narcissus, have a narcissus flower (commonly known as a daffodil) in the front of the room in a vase with a sign that says, "I wonder how this flower will be part of our learning today." The students will wonder, be entertained, and be surprised with the interest you have created, and will be more likely to remember the learning that day.

- **Stay one step ahead of the class.** One of the first times I wanted to read a novel with a class, I used the element of surprise. I had an underlying fear that some students would groan or roll their eyes when I announced the book title, not because it was an uninteresting book, but because with thirty-two students in the classroom, the odds were that this was likely to happen with at least two students. I decided to add surprise to make everyone, I sure hoped, excited.

    I found a shiny silver piece of cloth in a bin in my classroom. I piled up all of the student copies of the novel on the carpeted floor in front of the board. I draped the cloth over the pile, taped a piece of bright construction paper on top, and drew a huge question mark on it. The only way I can describe what happened when my eighth-grade students came into the room is this: Imagine a room full of flies and a big bowl of honey. They came and circled around the shiny lump, and I had to remind them many times not to touch it. This drove them crazy. A few put their heads to the carpet and tried to peek underneath the sheet; others tried to poke at it with a pencil (obeying the no-touch rule). "I think I know what it is, guys!" a student shrieked. Needless to say, when I whipped off the shiny cloth ten minutes into the lesson, I wanted them to sweat a bit; you could feel the excitement in the room about reading. They screamed, cheered, and could not wait to get their hands on the untouchable surprise object. Would I have had that engagement starting the same book by just passing it out? Of course not.

    The secret to being able to add the element of surprise is being one step ahead of the class. You have to know the next unit that you are going to teach, or how you will determine the winner in a class competition, or what novel you will read next. To sum up, the element of surprise not only adds fun and excitement to the classroom, it also shows the class that you are prepared, fun, and are in charge—a win-win situation.

Your turn

1. Think back to the last time somebody surprised you with something great. How did you feel building up to the surprise? How can the element of surprise increase engagement in the classroom?

   _____

   _____

   _____

   _____

2. Do you personally believe that the element of surprise can increase engagement? Why or why not?

   _____

   _____

   _____

   _____

3. Think back to a specific past lesson. How could you have incorporated a surprise to increase engagement or add excitement to the class?

   _____

   _____

   _____

   _____

Real Conversation With a Fifth-Grade Student

Teacher: Okay, yesterday the girls lined up first so today the boys line up first. It's 2017 and we're equalizing the genders.

Female Student: But they already get higher pay than we do!

PART 6
KEEPING YOURSELF SANE

Remembering a Teacher Who Hit Her Breaking Point

My first-grade teacher tied one of our classmates to his chair because he would keep getting up and running around while she was teaching. The boy would run around and hit people when we were quiet and listening to what she was teaching. She honestly just wanted him to sit in his chair so she could get through the lesson. Everybody in the class was pretty happy she did that. This was in the 1980s before anybody got in trouble for anything. She was a good teacher, too. She used something lying around. It wasn't like it was premeditated or anything. I think she was at her breaking point with him.

—Jenna, age 38

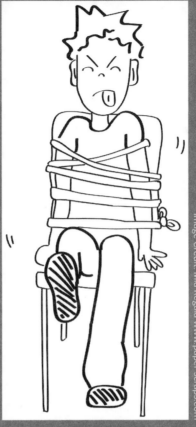

Image Credit: Mia Regala www.paper-scraps.com

How does keeping yourself sane relate to classroom management?

The goal is that we don't want to reach our own breaking point. Keeping yourself sane is all about controlling the amount of stress we bring into our lives during the school year. We don't want to have the urge to tie our students to their chairs. Even the best teachers can hit their breaking point if they don't take care of themselves throughout the school year mentally and physically. In this section, I'll explain a few key ways to keep yourself healthy so you can give your best self to your students. When you take shortcuts with your own self care, it reflects in your teaching. You won't have as much patience, energy, and enthusiasm with your students.

I REMEMBER WHEN. . . .

I remember when the train station was in complete chaos. It was the fall of 2005, and I was expecting my quiet commute to my school in the Paris suburbs, but the trains were stopped.

Some commuter trains had been vandalized in protest of a deadly incident that led to a state of emergency and violent rioting in France. Two immigrant teenagers had been unjustly electrocuted while running from local police, and the immigrant community was angry over years of ongoing issues surrounding immigration.

I had come to the City of Light to learn about second language education as a Fulbright Exchange teacher. After three years of teaching middle and high school French in the United States, I wanted to see how languages were taught in Europe, and drink coffee in cute cafes on the side. I was assigned to a middle school in the Parisian suburbs. But, voila! I found myself teaching in the heart of a national issue.

The next few weeks were difficult and beautiful as I navigated this unforeseen situation. Ten years later, as a teacher, I see where I failed and succeeded in trying to keep the learning going in my classroom during this national crisis.

My first mistake was that I had expectations. I was a skilled, hard-working teacher and assumed I would have another smooth year. Never did I imagine circumstances powerful enough that I could not fight through them. Let go of expectations of what type of school year you will have.

Second, I blamed myself for what happened in my classroom after the rioting began, rather than taking a look at the bigger picture. What I know now is that we can't always be perfect. Sometimes, a misbehaving class is a result of something larger going on. My school was comparable to an inner-city school in the United States. Add a national crisis, and some days I could not teach a single lesson to my chaotic classes. I felt guilty and unqualified as my students' learning halted.

I should have allowed myself room to fail forward during this time. Even the seasoned French teachers struggled to manage their classrooms.

The one thing I'm proud of during this time was the fact that I reached out for help. As teachers, sometimes we can't do it completely alone. I talked to my local American friends about my anxiety, and they fed me dinners as they took time to deepen my understanding of the history of immigrant issues. I kept in touch with my teaching mentor in the United States to get moral support. I asked my French colleagues for help with classroom management. Teachers are caregivers, and we need to support each other.

On my days off from school, I took advantage of what only Paris could offer. I played duets with a violinist friend, and frequented French movies, small concerts, and museums. I ate as well as I could with my anxious nerves, and walked all over exploring the city for exercise. We teach from the overflow of a full life, and I did the things I love to do.

To do this job, we need to preserve the peace inside of ourselves. My biggest success was that upon my return to my school in the United States, I saw the incredible value in my teaching role amidst my simple, peaceful community. A teacher plays an irreplaceable part in maintaining a stable community. We teach, we nurture, and we inspire to preserve peace and prosperity. It might sound cliché, but we need to keep our cups full to pour into students, for the future is formed in our classrooms.

—Rebekah Madren
High School French Teacher
Patuxent River, Maryland
15 years' experience
Fulbright Scholar

Balance Your Life

You can't pour from an empty cup.

—Anonymous

It took me four years to get this. In my first year teaching, my principal found me one Friday evening around 8:30 p.m. in my classroom working. When he entered, I was secretly excited that he could see how dedicated I was. He stuck in only his head said two words: "Go home." This habit of staying late into the night in my classroom lasted my first few years. In addition to the many hours at school, I exercised rarely, often worked late into the night, ate poorly, and just did not take care of myself. What happened? I snapped at my class when they misbehaved, did not have the energy they needed, and became more and more worn down.

The bottom line is the title of this part of the book. In order for you to take care of your classroom, you have to take care of yourself. Eat right, exercise, and get enough sleep. It's easier said than done, especially if you have a family at home. The point is that there has to be a body-mind-spirit balance. I was unbalanced my first few years. After I made a conscious effort to balance my life, I noticed that my teaching improved dramatically.

I was the best teacher I could be when I had balance. Students deserve a teacher who is healthy and rested. I was working hard, but also got into an exercise routine, was going to bed at a reasonable hour, and was conscious about what food was going into my body. Face it; you have to be in tip-top mental shape to win this race. So how do you do it? Do you just not finish all of the work for your classroom?

Tips for Keeping Your Balance

- **Exercise.** Schedule exercise into your calendar. There will always be something that comes up, but exercise! Whether it is walking, running, yoga, Pilates, or your home treadmill, do it at least twice a week. It will come in handy when Juan has banged on the desk one too many times. Instead of losing your cool, you will notice that you will actually have patience.

- **Keep one Get Out of Jail Free card.** Shhhh . . . this one is a secret and only to be used once in a while when you're really in a bind. Is there something that has been sitting on your desk, waiting to be graded, for more than three weeks? Chances are the students do not remember. Realize that you will never be able to grade everything. Focus on the present assignments that specifically assess essential skills that link to the standards. Is there a pile of papers that don't necessarily link to a standard, or have you already graded another assignment that assesses the same skill? Skip grading these and move forward. This will free your mind for more relevant assignments. Skipping a hurdle or two can help you win the overall race. It's okay, really.

- **Prioritize and prep!** Use your prep period to—prep! I make a list of what I have to do in my prep, put it on a sticky note, and stick to it; otherwise, I can get involved with one task too long. Prioritize what you have to do that will get you ahead. Make a list and stick to it.

- **Respond to correspondence immediately.** Respond to e-mails, papers, and phone calls as soon as possible. Once these start to build up, it's like credit card interest, and it will snowball. I used to get my mail and fill out the forms right in the mailroom to avoid creating a pile on my desk that was a visual stressor. Respond immediately if you can. This will also make you a more efficient and valuable employee.

- **Ask for student assistance sparingly.** It's okay to tell the students, if you are particularly tired or feeling ill one day, that you need their assistance to work with you. This will actually help you appear human in their eyes. However, if you overuse this, you will appear weak overall. Use this sparingly, very sparingly.

- **Separate your work life from your personal life.** In a 2014 study (Boch, 2014), Google attempted to answer the work-life balance question and conclude whether people were healthier who separated work and life— these people are known as "segmentors," or who integrated work and life—these people are known as "integrators." Google based the results of the study on measures of life satisfaction. They concluded that those who segmented were twice as happy as those who integrated.

This means you should develop interests out of work. Turn off your work e-mails when you are enjoying your own time. Schedule specific office hours on set days after school for your students to be able to contact you. Make time for you, so you can develop higher life satisfaction to be a better teacher for your students.

- **Focus on what matters most to you.** The bottom line is that we could all spend five or more straight years in our classroom and find things that need to be done, such as reorganizing cabinets, et cetera. What matters the most to you? For me, it was the lessons. I would perfect the plans, because I knew a tight and engaging lesson plan is the most effective way to minimize behavior issues in your classroom, which will help your mental well-being. Know that there are many distractions in the classroom, and you have to know what you *need* to get done, and how to do this and still manage time to take care of yourself.

The classroom can and will eat you alive if you do not take care of your emotional health, your physical health, and your overall well-being. You cannot use little time as an excuse. Make time. You can and you will be much happier and a better teacher for your students. They *will* notice a difference.

Your turn

1. Do you think it's possible to have a balanced work and personal life?

    _____

    _____

    _____

2. How balanced is your work and personal life right now?

    _____

    _____

    _____

3. Brainstorm and discuss specific changes that you want and need to make or make sure you keep.

    _____

    _____

    _____

4. Pull out your schedule, and schedule in activities that will preserve and balance your body, spirit, and mind and enable you to become a better teacher. Everybody wins.

    _____

    _____

    _____

Know How to Handle the Difficult Parent Meetings

We teachers all have these hard meetings and difficult parents. We get questioned, and we feel put on the defense sometimes, and chances are we will have to defend ourselves. We may have to rectify a situation. Difficult parent meetings are where our true strength comes out. They are where our words can be daggers or saviors, where we will see tears and laughs. Meetings are something we all mess up in, but through practice teachers can get better at handling difficult meetings.

I remember my first angry parent meeting. It was the last week of school. A girl in my class was upset because she felt that she deserved a higher grade. I was conducting the three-ringed circus I could call my classroom. Grades were already turned in, the students were finished with their work, and I was working to just keep them in their seats. A stranger's face appeared in the door. I could see the resemblance to the angry student. Was it her mother, her auntie, her grandmother? From the furious look on this powerful woman's face, it didn't matter. I was about to be told off, in front of my own class. What could I do? Call the office for help? Run? I was considering how far I could get.

In my attempt to remain professional and not hide under my desk like I wanted to, I asked her if we could step outside. I stepped away from the door so the students could not see her demeanor as she (I'm not sure how else to put it) told me off. Boy, did she let me have it. She angrily lectured me for what seemed like an eternity. Luckily, an administrator was walking by and entered the conversation to support me. I'm not sure what my class was doing besides listening as well as they could to their teacher being told off. After this meeting, I knew I had to make some changes. This could never be repeated. The biggest mistake was not informing the parent of the student's grade when it was starting to slip. I was just too busy, but I know now that it's essential to inform a parent when a student's grade is slipping quickly. Let's fast-forward to a meeting in my fifth year teaching:

A student in my class is frustrated with the grade she has earned. I know she received a low grade because she is talking too much in class and not doing her work to the best of her ability, but she feels she has been wronged. She has been venting to her parents, and her parents have asked her for a meeting with me.

Now, the first two rules are to not become defensive and to not become arrogant. Body language is important; give eye contact, and nod your head when they make a point. Do not cross your arms. Empathize with the parent. They love their child and will fight for what they think is right. It is not you they are angry with; it is the grade.

If a student mentions in class that their parent wants to speak to you, say to the student: Your parents would like a meeting with me? I think that's a good idea so we can see how to help you succeed.

Call the parent. Say to the parent, "Mr./Mrs. [parent's name]? This is Ms./Mr. [your name], the teacher of [student name] and I'm wondering if you have a moment?" (Respect their time.) "[Student name] mentioned to me that you would like a conference. I'm so glad she did because I was just about to call you. I'm glad we can work together to figure out the best way to help her. We both want her to succeed. When is a good time for you to come in?"

After you schedule the time, try to refrain from discussing any more on the phone; this can be handled during the conference. It is up to you, but I always preferred to have the student in the conference as well. She feels like she is part of the solution when she is given a chance to chime in and can be heard. After all, it is the student you are teaching every day, not the parent. I found these are the conferences that worked. Have documentation ready and prepare for the meeting; otherwise you will just be talking in circles. Have samples ready of student work and documentation of assignments not turned in, et cetera.

Okay, now at the conference be prepared, and know that the parent may come in angry and ready to fight. The goal of the conference is to listen, listen, listen. Empathize and diffuse. Do not go to a conference ready to win a fight; if you do, you'll have an angrier parent on your hands and administration involved, which is not what you want. Go in with the mindset that you are working on a collaborative solution for the student to succeed at school. Let's jump to the actual conference now:

Parent and student walk in. They both seem angry, ready to argue. You have bottled water ready for both, which surprises them. If it's chilled, brownie points! You have the student's grade already printed out (but flipped over so it doesn't upset her right away) and samples of her below-quality work. Show them that you are leading the meeting, but make sure they are heard. Here's how it could go:

Shake hands with both parent and student before you sit. "Mr. Smith, thank you so much for coming in today. I understand you are both concerned about Sarah's low grade. I am just as concerned. Sarah, could you tell us what is going on?"

Empower the student and let her talk. Do not interrupt; just listen. If she says something that is accusatory or just not accurate, respond with, "I'm sorry you feel that way."

Then, start your part with a student strength: "Sarah, I really value having you in class because you always raise your hand even when the others may not participate as much. It's nice to have a student as brave as you are in class every day." Think of at least one student strength before a meeting.

"However, sometimes you use that strength at inappropriate times. There have been times where we had to complete assignments and you were talking with a friend. This has caused a lower grade. Would you agree with that statement?" Most students would agree here. "So I would like to help you raise your grade. What can I do to help you talk less?"

The student will probably either shrug her shoulders or ask you to change her seat at this point. Most likely, the parent will probably jump in now and ask that you contact home if this happens again.

Bingo! You have just gotten what you need.

First of all, you empowered the parents. Now, when you call home the parents will most likely be on your side. Remember that the parents asked you to call home, so you'll be set. Second, the student knows that you and the parent are working together to help her. You just empowered both the student and the parent when they were originally coming in to fight. The student will most likely do better in class now without you ever having to call, or maybe you will need to make just an occasional phone call.

Tips for Successful Parent Meetings

- **Listen, listen, listen.** Show parents that you are listening by nodding your head yes. Put yourself in their shoes and understand their side. A parent wants to be heard and understood.

- **Be prepared with grades, work samples, and other documentation.** Use these as supports, not weapons.

- **Work *with* them.** Take the position that you are working *with* parents. You want the best for their child.

- **Come to an agreement.** Let the parent know you respect *their child*, and come to an agreement where you and the parent are working together for the student.

- **Schedule sooner than later.** It's much easier to be the first to bring attention to a situation in a meeting than to respond to an angry parent phone call. Parents will end up thanking you, rather than wondering why you've waited so long to call them. Remember that they love this child.

These tips could have saved me from wanting to hide under my desk.

Your turn

1. In your opinion, what is the biggest obstacle when it comes to working with parents? How can you overcome this obstacle?

    _____

    _____

    _____

    _____

2. Think back to a parent interaction that you have had that did not go as well as planned. With the knowledge you have now, is there anything you could have done differently to improve that interaction?

    _____

    _____

    _____

    _____

3. Now think back to a parent interaction that went exceptionally well. How did you contribute to this happening?

    _____

    _____

    _____

    _____

Keep it Balanced:
Give and Take Equally

When you are a teacher, you are part of a community, a school. As newer teachers, we are often in survival mode. This means we take all the help we can get. We take any worksheet that we can get. We try any lesson we can. We ask for help from anybody that will offer it. (You learn later to be picky about whom you ask, since you will get one hundred different answers.) We take to learn more. It's the nature of a new teacher. We are thirsty for help, and we need it. Help with anything from organization to time management to behavior management. However, there is a limit. We have to give back to the greater good.

Once you know what you are doing, start giving to others. Offer an ear when there is a crisis, coach a club or sport; offer to stay after school to help set up for an event; make copies for your partner teacher. Not only will it not tip the balance of the school as a whole, you never know when you will need a favor or help again from others. They'll remember that time you helped them out. Give and you shall receive. You do not want to be stranded on your own island without a boat.

Your turn

- Make a T-chart. Label one column "What I Give" and label the other column "What is Given to Me."

- Now, list as much as you can on each side. Be honest with yourself. Things you give or are given to you can be material, time, or support. Be specific.

- Look at your chart. Which way is it tipping? How can you add to the side that is underdeveloped to keep the scale even? List three specific ways you can even out your chart.

_____

_____

_____

_____

_____

BEST
PRACTICE
#49

Be Responsive
and Prioritize

Y ou get to school and have fifteen e-mails from coworkers, one from your
principal, and three from other teachers; responses needed to all immediately. I'm sweating just thinking about this. You also have a parent voicemail
waiting for a return call. A stack of paperwork is sitting on your desk from the
front office, not to mention your pile of papers to grade. Students are asking
every day when their grades will be updated, and you have yet to plan for next
week. How do you get it all done?

I struggled with this dilemma for years before I figured it out. The above
describes my life for four straight school years of teaching. Stress is caused
when you think about things you have to do. Stress creates a catch-22 situation,
because a stressed worker cannot perform at optimal level.

Tips for Responding and Prioritizing

- **Respond immediately.** Reply to e-mails as soon as you read them if possible. A pile of work is a visual and real stressor. You will be also known as
  an employee who gets things done if you keep up with paperwork. Do not
  let your pile go for more than two days if at all possible.

- **Complete your highest priority tasks first.** Prioritize. What really needs to
  get done right now? Do that.

- **Make a list.** Record what you have to do and then put it out of your mind. Carrying around what you have to do takes up valuable mental space and leaves less brainpower to actually complete your tasks. Check or erase tasks off your list as you complete them. This will give you a feeling of success.

- **Finish each task from beginning to end.** You will feel more of a sense of accomplishment from completing each task than doing lots of things halfway.

Your turn

1. What are the two most important work tasks that you have yet to do? List them and prioritize which is more important. Set a timeframe for when they will be completed.

    _____

    _____

    _____

2. Do the same for two personal tasks.

    _____

    _____

    _____

3. Was there anything you spent time on in the past at work that was unnecessary or held you back from other more important tasks? Looking back, how could you have reprioritized your responsibilities?

    _____

    _____

    _____

4. Do the same thinking for your personal tasks.

    _____

    _____

    _____

Be Mindful With Your Coworkers

Believe it or not, getting along with your coworkers is extremely important to your success inside the classroom and keeping yourself sane. The longer we teach, the more we realize that we absolutely do need our coworkers for support. Colleagues can cover a class, lend an extra ream of paper, cochaperone a field trip, help deal with a student, provide an experienced view on a difficult situation, cover you in a pinch when you have to use the restroom during class, or just provide emotional support for those challenging days. Burning bridges with a coworker can jeopardize your success as a teacher. Imagine being in a disagreement with another teacher one year, and then the next year being placed beside her classroom, or even being assigned to be her coteacher. Being on good terms with all of the employees at your school will help your personal career.

Golden Rules for Dealing With Coworker Conflict

1. Don't gossip.

2. Use a respectful tone when speaking to other adults.

3. If you mess up, apologize as soon as possible.

4. Resolve issues through conversation before they escalate.

5. Watch what you e-mail/post on social media. Consider it saved forever, and it can also be forwarded or shared with others.

6. Do not try to solve disagreements with a coworker over e-mail or text. If there is a disagreement or misunderstanding via e-mail or text, speak to the coworker in person as soon as possible to rectify the situation. Conversation is a priceless tool.

7. Use the chain of command. Always go to the coworker first, and then to the supervisor only if needed afterward. Supervisors should be used if the conflict cannot be resolved or if there is a legal issue involving a student or adult.

Your turn

1. Have you ever had a coworker gossip to you about another coworker? How did that make you feel, and what did that make you feel about the gossiping coworker?

    _____

    _____

    _____

    _____

2. As technology becomes the more acceptable means of communication, why is it important to remember that miscommunications and disagreements should always be handled in conversation, especially in the workplace?

    _____

    _____

    _____

    _____

3. Have you ever had a disagreement with a coworker or colleague? Was it resolved over conversation or by e-mail? Do you think this was the most effective medium for communication?

    _____

    _____

    _____

    _____

WIDENING OUR LENS: A GLOBAL PERSPECTIVE ON CLASSROOM MANAGEMENT

Classroom Management in Turkey

I remember when I began teaching first grade in Turkey. Most of the years I spent teaching at home were to middle school and high school students, and teaching younger students in a private school held a whole new set of challenges.

Typically, Turkish students feel pressured to be perfect in their work and exams, and many are fearful of making mistakes. In addition, classroom management is viewed as a tool for educators to point out how the student can improve, putting pressure on the student to be as perfect as possible. However, this is often done without motivation or encouragement, as these are seen as unuseful tools for success. This approach can be found in other classrooms around the world, but it is common in Turkey. To add to my students' pressure to be perfect, many of the parents in my school were doctors and owners of major companies. Teaching children in Turkey, I realized that motivation and encouragement are not commonly used in helping to guide people to learn and improve their work. After realizing this, I knew that I needed to do something to help my young students relax, have fun, and not put the main focus on being perfect.

My students were in need of a system to help provide this motivation. I felt it was important for me to teach them what it means to work for what they earn, to celebrate small successes, and the importance of earning privileges. I also felt the children who came from more privileged families could benefit from learning how to assimilate in the classroom and to see everyone, including themselves, as an equal without differentiation. At the same time, it would provide them with insight to see how to treat others properly, and it would reward them for modifying their behavior.

Turkey is known to be a very collective culture, where work is usually done together. I used reward systems to assist my students with developing their own identities, becoming more self-reliant, and doing things themselves with basic support. Furthermore, it taught them to be responsible for their own actions. This helped my young students to do better academically in the classroom and be good friends to their classmates. They started to succeed out of want of success, rather than fear of failure.

My rewards system created a much more positive classroom environment, more conducive to authentic learning. As with all things, I tested out many different methods until I found what really worked: I tried allowing them to choose avatars on Class Dojo (https://classdojo.zendesk.com) and featuring a star student of the week.

With Class Dojo, I give points to children individually dependent on their behavior in class each day, and for every ten points, I gave a series of rewards, beginning with a sticker or changing their dojo avatar, and going all the way up to being student helper and earning special certificates. If every student in the class received a dojo point on a given day, then the whole class received one dojo point, and for every ten points, the whole class received a whole class reward, beginning with ten minutes of free play time inside and outside and going all the way up to earning a class party.

Every week, I choose a new star student, giving each student in class a time to shine that week and be rewarded for their academic excellence and participation in class. I have a colorful poster where I put up photos of them, and they draw pictures around their photos to display "all about me" topics, such as their favorite subject in school or what they wanted to be when they grew up, et cetera.

As would be expected given the wide variety of personality traits among my students, and the facts that they were young and in the process of learning how to adapt to a classroom, I also ran into some complications with these reward systems and had to reflect on and find proper ways to solve these issues. Most kids at this age tend to be self-focused and can have a difficult time accepting and understanding when another child is rewarded, but they are not given the same thing. As expected, a few students got upset in the beginning because they were not given a sticker, or they were not able to be student of the week for a particular week. I didn't want any of my students to lose their motivation to earn rewards, and I didn't want to have any negative impact on the good relationship we had already built, so I decided to set some strategies in place to assist with this.

First, I made sure that every student in my class had a chance to be my star student of the week at some point during the whole school year, so that they would consistently stay motivated to participate and perform well in academics. As for the dojo points, when a student earned a reward, I brought the student to the front of the classroom to present the award, and I explained what behavior earned the reward, so the student was seen as a role model for other students to follow. I also awarded extra dojo points when I noticed extra efforts to do nice things for the classroom or for their friends or to help me. Students also learned to support each other and work collaboratively to earn Class Dojo points and class rewards.

After a period of consistency using the class rewards system, students who were once thinking that it was unfair that they did not receive the same rewards suddenly started to positively change their behavior and helped create a positive classroom environment along with their peers. I also started to notice extra efforts with answering questions and doing extra classwork, without much need for me to assist or intervene. After a while, the reward system on its own created a classroom environment that encouraged students to be more self-motivated, and they were actually happy for their friends who earned rewards. Using these reward systems has made a world of difference in my classrooms, and the children really feel more self-accomplished and responsible, and they develop an understanding of their ability to achieve and succeed. I have really found these systems to be highly effective and recommend other school teachers use a similar system for a happy academic and behavioral learning environment.

—Samantha Reinblatt
7 years' teaching in Istanbul
Üsküdar SEV American School

Your turn

1. What conclusions can we draw from this teacher's international experience with classroom management?

_____

_____

_____

_____

2. What performance problem was the main obstacle (from Best Practice #9) in this teacher's classroom for whole student success, and how did this teacher overcome it?

_____

_____

_____

_____

3. Would you have done the same? Why or why not?

_____

_____

_____

_____

Handy To-Go List of 50 Teaching Dos and Don'ts

MAGIC WANDS OF TEACHING	DEADLY SINS OF TEACHING
1. Learn student names as fast as possible.	1. Students realizing that you do not know their names as the school year progresses.
2. Be the teacher you are.	2. Not letting students see much of your personality.
3. Set routines and structures early, even before they are needed.	3. Waiting until routines and structures are needed before creating them.
4. Use "I" statements. *Examples*: "I need you to. . . ." "Do me a favor and. . . ."	4. Using you-statements. *Example:* "You need to. . . ."
5. Use student data to create a purposeful seating chart early in the year.	5. Making a seating chart without using student data.
6. Praise the positive often.	6. Focusing on the negative behaviors in a classroom.
7. Redirect encouragingly when students make mistakes.	7. Shaming students for making mistakes.
8. Speak to the tough students using the same tone you use with other students.	8. Speaking to the tough students in a different tone than you use with the other students.
9. Become a teacher detective when students are not performing.	9. Assuming that the students "do not want to learn" when the students aren't performing.
10. Use your words and tone to give a positive and caring energy to your classroom.	10. Using your words and tone to send a negative energy through the classroom often.
11. Focus on the positive with the full class, and address the negative *privately* with students one on one.	11. Disciplining publically, often; it will give you only a false sense of power.
12. Connect with the most challenging and withdrawn students by finding out what interests them.	12. Assuming the challenging students are just always going to be challenging.
13. Reward students.	13. Telling a class of students that they do not deserve a reward.
14. Use behavior contracts for your most challenging students.	14. Continuing with the same consequences for your most challenging students.
15. Connect your curriculum to the real world.	15. Not connecting your curriculum with the world.
16. Stay up-to-date on current teaching practices by reading teaching books and attending conferences.	16. Doing the same thing every year.
17. Keep the pace up: Use ten- to twenty-minute chunks in your lesson plans for elementary and middle school, and thirty- to forty-minute chunks for high school.	17. Teaching too slowly.

(Continued)

(Continued)

MAGIC WANDS OF TEACHING	DEADLY SINS OF TEACHING
18. Use arm's length voice with students.	18. Speaking so every student in the classroom can hear you when you are working with students in small groups or one on one.
19. Do a mental dry run of your lesson to find any holes and identify any necessary last-minute preparation.	19. Not having a lesson plan prepared before class.
20. Try project- or problem-based units during the year.	20. Spending most of the year not tying the curriculum into the bigger picture.
21. Make your curriculum challenging, and include academic scaffolds for support daily.	21. Making your curriculum too easy or too challenging without support.
22. Take risks in your lessons.	22. Always keeping students in their comfort zone.
23. Prepare your students for success when you will not be there.	23. Missing many days of work.
24. Use creative discipline once in a while.	24. Never letting your creative or fun side show in your class.
25. Use nonverbal cues to keep students silent during a test or silent reading.	25. Talking in a classroom that is supposed to be silent.
26. Prepare students for groupwork by giving them a clear written description of the task and giving each one an individual role (if needed).	26. Not communicating clear tasks for groupwork.
27. Have creative and well-planned lessons.	27. Having dry and unprepared lessons often.
28. Include at least three types of engagement styles in each lesson.	28. Having only one engagement style in your lesson.
29. If a lesson flops, use it as learning tool by spending time reflecting on what could have been done differently.	29. Not taking the time to reflect if a lesson flops.
30. Know that even difficult parents are acting out of love and concern.	30. Becoming defensive when parents are difficult.
31. Take the time to plan with your coteacher.	31. Hoping coteaching will just work out without planning or communication.
32. Ask for help when needed.	32. View asking for help as a weakness.
33. Find a mentor who is better than you at teaching.	33. Never spending time observing teachers who are better than you at teaching.
34. Ask other teachers if you may observe their classes, if only for a few minutes.	34. Never taking the time to observe other teachers.
35. When talking to a group of teachers, take mental notes about what you can try in your own class.	35. Only telling stories of your own classroom with other teachers.
36. Speak about your students respectfully.	36. Constantly expressing that your students don't want to learn.
37. Invite relevant guest speakers into your classroom, and prepare students for the visit.	37. Not preparing your students for a guest speaker.
38. Incorporate student voices in lessons daily.	38. Always keeping control of the classroom by silencing students and valuing teacher voice.
39. Show students you care in your actions.	39. Only telling students you care with words.

MAGIC WANDS OF TEACHING	DEADLY SINS OF TEACHING
40. Laugh with your class.	40. Keeping your class serious all of the time.
41. Give gifts.	41. Telling your students they don't deserve anything.
42. Create an emotionally safe learning environment from Day 1.	42. Reacting strongly when students make mistakes, keeping them afraid to take risks in your classroom.
43. Keep your class clean and organized, and display pictures of your students.	43. Letting your classroom stay unorganized and cluttered.
44. Be prepared for success when covering a class.	44. Expecting that students will misbehave when covering a class.
45. Once in a while, add the element of surprise to your lessons to increase engagement and vitality in your classroom.	45. Never including surprises in your lessons.
46. Schedule exercise into your calendar, especially during the school year.	46. Not making time to take care of yourself.
47. Be prepared for difficult parent meetings.	47. Showing up at a difficult parent meeting unprepared.
48. Give and take equally in your professional environment.	48. Giving too much or taking too much in your professional environment.
49. Complete your high-priority tasks first, and complete each task from beginning to end when possible.	49. Not prioritizing your tasks.
50. Use conversation, not e-mail or text, to connect and resolve minor conflicts with coworkers.	50. Gossiping about coworkers.

The End—of
the Beginning

T he end of the beginning is a great place to be. When you do not have to spend countless hours picking up paper balls after class or calling parents for negative behavior, you can actually start getting creative without fear. It's a beautiful thing to focus your precious time writing lesson plans knowing the class is on your side, not your enemy at war. I sometimes have posttraumatic first-year flashbacks where I remember the boy rocking side to side and the class seeming more threatening than any war fought over the past hundred years.

A talented ninth-grade teacher who later transitioned into administration once told me something that stuck. She said the goal of a teacher by the end of the year is to "teach herself out of a job." This means you've created a real community of learners that depend on each other, and not you, for help. This means they can resolve small conflicts, they can stay motivated without constant redirection, they can collaborate and share confidently within their groups, and they demonstrate higher-order thinking skills.

I can always gauge a successful school year if the kids don't notice when I walk out of the room because they are too engaged in their learning and with each other in academic collaboration. They are usually in project- or problem-based learning units, and, as my mentor used to say, "on auto-pilot." Sometimes, the last month of school, I'll test this, walk a few feet out past the classroom door, and wait. Usually, they don't notice I walked away because they are too engaged in their final projects. They also don't need me to resolve minor conflicts, because they have learned these skills. They also don't depend on me for constant praise, because they have developed their own sense of self-esteem. Those moments are when I get shivers and my eyes may even tear up a bit, because as teachers we get emotional when we have moments like this. We just do. I feel like this because I know they have a much better chance of being fine out there in the real world if they don't need me anymore. It's a bittersweet feeling that we'll all experience. Most years I've gotten these results, but not every year, because we're teachers and we're human. If we don't get this result at the end of a school year, it's okay, because the times we do, it's phenomenal. And we will get this result most years.

Okay, so I'm no longer a soldier at war, or a drill sergeant even. I am a teacher through and through, and the students and I are side by side on this learning journey. There are many things I still have to learn, and I work on them daily. How do I use technology in the classroom to maximize learning and increase engagement? How do I challenge the most gifted child without separating him from the class? How do I work with adults as successfully as children? These questions are what push me every day to become better at my chosen profession. I use my own experience to listen, to keep learning, and to find mentors. One of the most beautiful aspects of teaching is that we are always learning. We are always growing as teachers, and our students are always growing.

Good luck in your journey and perhaps we will meet someday, somewhere along our paths. Here's to you and your dreams; I hope sharing my real experiences helped you reach a little higher.

—Serena

Real Advice: Teacher to Teacher

Every day's a new day. Always give your students the opportunity to make good choices. Be flexible; things happen, and go with the flow. Smile and show students that you care; you may be the only person who does. Also, be calm and patient.

Ms. Saft, 6 years' experience, Early Childhood Education Specialist, Kimbrough Elementary School, California

In many cases, teaching can be and often is stressful. There are days when you will be angry, frustrated, anxious, and emotional. Do something about it. Take a break, write about your feelings in a journal, go to the movies, the theater, et cetera. Most important, do something physical; try yoga, take a long walk, jog, or work in your yard.

Dr. DeRoche, 30 years' experience, Former Middle School Teacher and Principal, University of San Diego, California

As teachers, we cannot fully understand our students until we put ourselves in their shoes.

Ms. Hambira, 15 years' experience, High School Teacher, Kgari Sechele Senior Secondary School, Botswana

I think one of the most powerful behavior management techniques is for the students to like you and want to be in your class. I always work on that first, making the class a fun and loving place to be. If students like you and respect you, then they care what you think and want to please you. If you teach through intimidation and fear, you may get temporary results, but at what price?

Mrs. Perez, 21 years' experience, Kindergarten Teacher, Jefferson Elementary School, California

Project-based learning allows students to become aware of the benefits of working together in this world, allowing for peace not only to be possible, but inevitable.

Mr. Kemp, 10 years' experience, High School Teacher, Vista High School, California

Take time to get to know each student personally—greet each one by name every day while smiling and looking them in the eyes; talk to each student when you have a chance and listen to them without judging. Be your authentic self, and don't be afraid to share a little of who you are with your students. Then you will have real relationships with your students, you will be happier in the classroom, and you will find you have fewer disciplinary issues.

Mrs. Swan-Gerstein, 11 years' experience, Former Elementary Vice Principal, Integral Elementary School, California

Be yourself. Don't be afraid to laugh at yourself in front of the students. Admit when you are wrong, but always be firm, consistent, and fair, and love them.

Mrs. Mello, 11 years' experience, Middle and Elementary School Teacher, Golden Hill Elementary School, California

Don't judge someone on who she is when she is thirteen. We never know what path each kid will eventually take, and we have to try our best to be a nice stop on the path. It's taken me a long time to figure that out. Also, start fresh every day. Don't hold grudges. Pacing helps classroom management, too. I try to change activities every ten to fifteen minutes to keep minds active and engaged.

Mrs. Register, 10 years' experience, Middle and High School Teacher, Cajon Park School, California

It's important to cultivate an atmosphere in which mutual respect is practiced. You listen to and respect the students' voices, and they show each other and you respect. They don't have to like everyone or you, but they need to practice respect. The working world needs people who will work with others to get the job finished. Prepare your lessons well. The best prevention is a well-prepared lesson.

Mrs. Pariser, 34 years' experience,
Retired High School Alternative Education
Teacher, Hampdon Academy, Maine

One thing that helped me a lot is being prepared: lesson plans, planning, resources. Remember you are there to teach and not to gain popularity or friendship. Popularity comes from having your learners intrigued, which comes from being prepared and going the extra mile, especially as a new teacher.

Mr. Sawyers, 5 years' experience,
Middle and High School Teacher,
Windhoek High School, Namibia

The result of imposed authority by teachers is reflected in student behavior when you ask them to teach junior [younger] students. Senior [older] students are found to be more focused on maintaining discipline by using elevated voice pitch than on attaining the learning outcomes of the assigned task. Some of our seniors [eighth-grade students] were assigned a task to teach juniors [third-grade students]. They were as rude or as kind as their teachers. It was like "monkey do what monkey sees."

Mr. Sijapati, 9 years' experience, Elementary and Middle School Administrator and Teacher, Creative Academy, Nepal

It can be overwhelming with trivial details when organizing your classroom at the beginning of the school year. Make it your own! Do what works for you. For example, if having space on the floor for students to work on their bellies using clipboards is important to you, then be sure to have an area for floor work.

Ms. Vaites, 21 years' experience, Elementary School Teacher, Greenfield Middle School, Massachusetts

The first year teaching first grade was a real challenge, as I hadn't yet figured out the key to proper classroom management skills. But, as with all things, I tested out many different methods until I found what really worked. Using reward systems, like Class Dojo, has made a world of difference in my classrooms, and the children really feel more self-accomplished and responsible, and they develop an understanding of their ability to achieve and succeed.

Ms. Reinblatt, 7 years' experience, Early Elementary School ESL Teacher, Uskudar SEV American School, Turkey

What's worked for me, with connecting with students, is understanding they are already very accomplished people. I don't tell them what to do and what not to do. I share my stories and listen to their goals and dreams. While listening to them, I don't judge. Listening helps me to deeply connect.

Ms. Rai, 5 years' experience, Inspirational Youth Speaker, India

Do everything you can in the beginning of the year to create a sense of community within your classroom. This takes time at first but goes a long way when your students feel ownership of the room and group!

Mrs. Pariser, 8 years' experience,
Elementary School Teacher/Counselor,
Akiba Schechter Day School, Illinois

Identify a student in the classroom who's a leader, even if the student leads in a negative way. Get to know that student and become friends—get the student on your side. Then the other kids will follow!

Jackie Hicks, 10 years' experience,
Middle and High School Teacher,
Cortez Hill Academy, California

Make sure to practice self care and nurture your needs as a person. It's important to identify passions outside of teaching and continue to pursue those as well. I now get monthly massages and pedicures; I practice meditation and being present in the moment; and I do things I love that make me feel most alive, such as writing poetry and going to the beach, concerts, and farmers' markets. When you honor your own needs, it allows you to feel more whole, therefore making you a better teacher for your students.

Mrs. Zimmermaker, 9 years' experience,
Education Specialist, Mesa Verde
Middle School, California

In my second year of teaching, I decided to take a different approach to that of the traditional authoritative teacher; I was enthusiastic, kind, and positive. I resolved not to raise my voice. As a result, I found that my students became more kind, positive, and enthusiastic as well.

Mrs. Beck, 7 years'
experience, Middle and High
School Teacher, Gompers
Preparatory Academy, California

Real Conversation With an Elementary School Student

Me [introducing myself to a very young student I didn't know]: Hello. My name is Ms. Pariser. If you can't remember that you are welcome to call me Ms. P for today. P like Potato. Can you repeat my name back to me?

Student: Your name is Potato.

Bibliography
and References

Achor, S. (2010). *The happiness advantage.* New York: Random House.

Adams, S. (2014). The 10 skills employers most want in 2015 graduates. *Forbes.* https://www.forbes.com/sites/susanadams/2014/11/12/the-10-skills-employers-most-want-in-2015-graduates/#7275c89e2511

Boch, L. (2014). Google's scientific approach to work-life balance (and much more). *Harvard Business Review.* https://hbr.org/2014/03/googles-scientific-approach-to-work-life-balance-and-much-more

Carnegie, D. (1981). *How to win friends and influence people.* New York: Pocket Books.

Child Trends Inc. (2015, June). Key "soft skills" that foster youth workforce success: Toward a consensus across fields. *Workforce Connections.* https://www.childtrends.org/wp-content/uploads/2015/06/2015-24AWFCSoftSkillsExecSum.pdf

DeRoche, E. (2013, November 12). *The skills game* [Blog post]. http://sites.sandiego.edu/character/blog/2013/11/12/skills-game/

Faith, R. (2017). How to create a behavioral contract with your teen. *How to Adult.* http://howtoadult.com/behavioral-contract-teen-2221199.html

Fletcher, A (2015). *Multiple engagement styles.* https://soundout.org/multiple-engagement-styles/

Kelly, W. M. (2003). *Rookie teaching for dummies.* New York: Wiley.

Lippmann, L., Ryberg, R., Carney, R., & Moore K. (2015). *Key "soft skills" that foster youth workforce success: Toward a consensus across fields.* Bethesda, MD: Child Trends.

Mager, R., & Pipe, P. (1997). *Analyzing performance problems.* Atlanta: CEP Press.

Musiowsky-Borneman, T. (2016). *Co-teaching: It's a marriage.* http://inservice.ascd.org/co-teaching-its-a-marriage/

Multiple intelligences: What does the research say? (2016, July 20). *Edutopia.* https://www.edutopia.org/multiple-intelligences-research

Pariser, S. (2015). *Let students make mistakes!* http://edtrans.org/let-students-make-mistakes-serena-pariser/

Robinson, K. (2007). *Do schools kill creativity?* [TED video]. https://www.ted.com/talks/ken_robinson_says_schools_kill_creativity

Smith, D. (2015). *Better than carrots or sticks.* Alexandria, VA: ASCD.

Steward, J. (2013, March 16). Looking for a lesson in Google's perks. *New York Times.* http://www.nytimes.com/2013/03/16/business/at-google-a-place-to-work-and-play.html?mcubz=3

Suttie, J. (2015, April 24.). Why humans need surprise. *Greater Good Magazine.* https://greatergood.berkeley.edu/article/item/why_humans_need_surprise

Teaching & Learning Transformation Center, University of Maryland. (n.d.). *Creating effective group work: Tips, tricks and resources.* University of Maryland http://smartgrowth.umd.edu/assets/pals/group_work_handout.pdf

Thiagarajan, S. (2006). *Thiagi's 100 favorite games*. San Francisco: Pheiffer.

Urban, H. (2004). *Positive words, powerful results.* New York: Simon & Shuster.

Walker, R. (2014). *Why do children misbehave?* http://www.valleychildtherapy.com/why_do_children_misbehave.html

Wilson, L. (2017). *Madeline Hunter lesson plan model.* http://thesecondprinciple.com/teaching-essentials/models-of-teaching/madeline-hunter-lesson-plan-model/

Wright, J. (n.d.). *Behavior contracts.* Intervention Central. http://www.interventioncentral.org/behavioral-interventions/challenging-students/behavior-contracts

Index

CORWIN
A SAGE Publishing Company

Helping educators make the greatest impact

Carol Pelletier Radford

The support you need for mindful mentoring and sustainable teacher success.

Carol Pelletier Radford

Use this resource to proactively prepare for your first few years in the classroom.

Jonathan Eckert

Discover how to teach with the daring of a beginner and a lifelong passion for learning and growth.

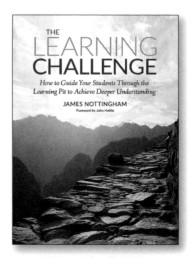

James Nottingham

Embrace challenge and encourage your students to dive into the "learning pit" to discover their eureka moment.

Corwin books represent the latest thinking from some of the most respected experts in K–12 education. We are proud of the breadth and depth of the books we have published and the authors we have partnered with in our mission to better serve educators and students.

Heather Wolpert-Gawron

Use these 10 strategies to teach and communicate with students when they're collaborating, talking, and working with their peers.

Ana Homayoun

Solutions for students to navigate and manage distractions in an ever-changing social media world.

Lisa Johnson

Building 21st century communication skills by helping educators design authentic learning experiences.

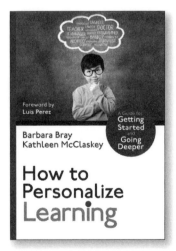

Barbara Bray, Kathleen McClaskey

Create a powerful shift in education by building a culture of learning so every learner is valued.

A SAGE Publishing Company

Helping educators make the greatest impact

CORWIN HAS ONE MISSION: to enhance education through intentional professional learning.

We build long-term relationships with our authors, educators, clients, and associations who partner with us to develop and continuously improve the best evidence-based practices that establish and support lifelong learning.

Solutions you want. Experts you trust.
Results you need.